To Barbara Gray —

who has h

D0885891

INSIDER SECRETS TO WINNING
YOUR PERSONAL INJURY BATTLE

A Seasoned Trial Lawyer Reveals All

*with thanks
for your interest in
my work —*

ALBERT M. STARK

Albert Stark

Copyright © 2009

All rights reserved. No part of this book may be reproduced or transmitted in any form or by any means, electronic or mechanical, including photocopying, recording, or by any information storage or retrieval system without permission in writing from the copyright owner.

ISBN# 978-0-9844646-0-9 0-9844646-0-3

This book was printed in the United States of America.

To order additional copies of this book, visit:
www.InsidersSecretsToWinning.com
www.personalinjury411.com
www.survivalfortheseriouslyinjured.com

Riverdel Press L.L.C.

TO NANCY KARLOSKY

and

FLORANCE CHURCHILL

Contents

INTRODUCTION

This book is about looking back at cases of seriously injured people, seeing what their lives are like many years later, how they managed their lives, finding out if the money they received helped them, learning about what they did right—and wrong.

The events and circumstances in this book are based on real cases that I have handled myself or with lawyers at the Stark & Stark law firm. I have used actual names, places and locations in many instances. I have used fictitious names or places or locations and combined cases where I felt it necessary or more appropriate to do so. The substitutions and combinations do not alter the significance of the book. The cases teach many lessons, not only to those who face challenges they never dreamed of confronting, but also to the millions who treat the seriously injured as a silent minority.

Going to court with hundreds of seriously injured persons, I have witnessed the hurdles they had to jump to get justice. Large injury verdicts have become media events and the subjects of well-known movies. News channels like CNN, MSNBC and Fox inaccurately report cases, calling the winners of multi-million dollar verdicts "lottery winners," polluting the airwaves and people's minds with stories of frivolous lawsuits, and blaming the legal system and "the litigious society in which we live" for exorbitant insurance premiums and healthcare costs. Laws limiting victims' rights under the guise of tort reform put a stumbling block in front of innocent citizens.

Is winning big in court a lottery? My clients answer—Telling the truth about what is behind those million dollar verdicts. Their stories show what it takes to fight insurance companies, what happens to seriously injured people after the court case is over. They even suggest how our court system can be reformed so that going to court isn't hell.

My clients' stories demonstrate the importance of competent physicians, therapists, financial advisors and—yes, lawyers, who passionately represent people others look away from or give up on, people who are brain injured, burned or paralyzed—yes, lawyers who are a detective, social worker, engineer, financial advisor, storyteller, producer and director, and, of course, an actor.

My clients show what it takes to go home, what it is like to be institutionalized, and what brain, burn and spinal cord injuries require. Their inspirational stories are about frustration and anger, courage and bravery— hope and reality.

Growing up, the spotlight shone on my father, a respected lawyer. He wanted me to follow in his footsteps. I did not want to walk in his shadow so I enrolled in a pre-med course at Dartmouth College in Hanover, New Hampshire in 1956. His dad—Grandpa Lou—who said his last goodbye two years before, would have been thrilled.

In spite of or maybe because he had a difficult life, Grandpa Lou had a favorite expression, "To understand the other guy, you have to walk a mile in his shoes." About five-feet-five inches tall, he loved to show me the biceps that bulged when he flexed his arms. "Put up your dukes," he'd say. "Let's see how tough you are." A skilled heart surgeon gave Grandpa Lou the second aortic transplant in the world. It kept him alive for eleven years—long enough to see his Brooklyn Dodgers win another World Series and his grandson win his first tennis tournament.

From college, I wrote Grandma Raschkow, my mother's mother, a letter in which I explained that I wanted to help people like Grandpa Lou and signed it "Albert Stark F.M.D" (Future Medical Doctor). She said, "Do something else, anything else. Don't be meshuggana. (Yiddish for crazy). Vith hands like you have, you shouldn't be a doctor." Grandma Raschkow, an accomplished seamstress, had tried many times to teach me to thread a needle. She had learned from her failures.

I should have followed her advice. The dogfish I dissected in introductory zoology looked as if it had been through a grinder. I scrambled the egg from which I had tried to extract an embryo. After I was the only student in analytic chemistry that could not mix chemicals precisely enough to measure the size of molecules, I made my first lawyer call to my father. I had switched to pre-law.

The next summer, in California for a national tennis tournament, I was impressed with a part of the country ripe for growth. Ambitious to plant my mark on the frontier, I returned to school. In college and law school, I took every state and local government and land development course offered. When I was about to graduate from law school, Governor John Love of Colorado, who was developing a water resource plan to spur growth in his state, offered me a job. But after a law school professor brought my college thesis and law school articles about urban redevelopment of northeastern cities to the attention of New Jersey Governor Richard J. Hughes, he recruited me. Hughes was my father's friend and colleague. He wanted legislation drafted that would enable New Jersey's cities to replace slums with low and moderate-income housing and create a department of community affairs. After he called Governor Love, he assured me that the Colorado job would not be filled for a year. I unpacked my bags. I completed my work for Hughes in four months. Then Trenton's mayor hired me to bring the city's ordinances up to date to take advantage of the laws I had just written.

I was born and reared in Trenton, playing touch football and stoopball in the street, swimming in the canal that ran past my house and attending public schools that rivaled the best private ones. But over the years, labor unions had chased away the industries that earned Trenton its motto "Trenton Makes the World Takes." Unemployment soared and housing deteriorated. Whites sent their children to private schools and the public schools were becoming blackboard jungles. The canal with weeping willows and dogwoods lining its banks was now a ribbon of concrete. Trenton was well on its way to becoming a ghetto island surrounded by a sea of suburbia.

While I was working for the mayor, an impatient Governor Love filled the Colorado position, so I set up shop in an empty room at my father's office. My first client was a city planner who was building apartment buildings for senior citizens and moderate and low-income families. I met Ellen in New York while I studied housing projects in Harlem and we married in November 1966.

On October 24, 1967 at eight-thirty in the morning, I hustled Ellen through a door at Mercer Hospital labeled "Maternity." I looked forward to one of the brightest days of my life. Twelve hours later, the obstetrician sat down next to me in the Father's Waiting Room and said, "You are the father of a baby boy." But her voice was solemn. "I had trouble," she said. Instead of a Caesarian delivery, which Ellen's condition dictated, the obstetrician had delivered an almost ten-pound baby naturally and now Ellen had no feeling in her right leg and my son's right arm didn't move.

I had until this moment led a relatively smooth life. It was dark outside and inside the apartment to which I returned. My heart was tight as a fist. I knelt and screamed, "I want to die," smashing my forehead on the bathtub.

Over the next four months, we all traveled back and forth to the Rusk Rehabilitation Institute at New York University Medical Center. Helpless, I had to surrender my wife and son to doctors. I met families with children disabled by birth-related conditions that needed extensive physical care, supervision, and support. The parents felt they would be "bad parents" if they "abandoned" their child to large state institutions, the only option for care at that time. Social workers warned them not to be "saints or martyrs," urging them not to take the child home. Caring for a child with severe disability, they were told, would be physically and emotionally draining, every day would be a new trial, every action, even those performed habitually and unconsciously in the past, would be an accomplishment as difficult as climbing to the summit of Mount Everest. I didn't know it then that my experience would help me walk in other person's shoes in the years to come.

My waiting room buddies at Rusk had loved ones who had been brain-injured, burned, or paralyzed, many of them in accidents. They were suing. They experienced improvement and hope at Rusk but setbacks and disappointment with their lawsuits. I never thought of suing our doctor for failing to do the Caesarian section in what was a "slam dunk" malpractice case because she was a close family friend. After a few of my new buddies found out that I was a lawyer, an urban development lawyer, not an accident lawyer, they confided things I could not imagine happening to me.

"My ambulance chaser is just out for his one-third."

"I had to fight with insurance companies to get medical treatment."

"Going to court was hell."

The disabled people and families had found a sympathetic ear. All of them respected doctors, but they didn't like lawyers.

Fortunately, Ellen and Jared regained almost total use of their injured limbs. During their nine-month home rehabilitation program, I read one neurology book after another, giving myself an education I thought was needed only in my personal life.

On April 4, 1968, Martin Luther King was assassinated. Four days later, catastrophe struck downtown Trenton, pillaged and burned by rioting high school students. Businesses that were spared fled to the suburbs. My clients lost interest in Trenton's future. What Trenton was a day before it no longer was. Trenton had become a seriously injured city.

Rachel was born with a normal delivery in October 1969. I had a wife and children to support and the urban development team I was putting together had no source for funding.

That's when Bobbie McKenzie called. Bobbie had been my boss during college summers when I was on the maintenance crew at Trenton, New Jersey's tennis courts. Three days before Bobbie's friend called me, Bobbie had been badly hurt in some kind of accident. I went to the hospital as a pal, but that visit propelled me toward a career as an advocate for the seriously injured—people who in a millisecond had become different people. Who they were before they were no longer.

My experience with serious injury cases during the next forty years would show me that Grandpa Lou's heart surgeon had a fairly straightforward job.

Certainly, operating on people's hearts is exceedingly difficult but once the heart is replaced or repaired and is working, he could go on to the next patient. Because serious injury cases are seldom, if ever, over, I would learn that it would be hard, but necessary, to continue to walk in my client's shoes.

Bobbie turned his head on the pillow. "Over here," he said, motioning with an arm wired with intravenous tubes. He introduced me to his wife, Roann, a buxom redhead in her late thirties. With her lips painted a bright red, she could be perfectly cast as a waitress at a roadside diner. "Oh, man, it hurts," Bobbie said, closing his eyes.

"Bobbie's going to need months of rehabilitation. I don't know how I'm going to handle this. Who's going to pay the doctors?" Roann said.

She told me what had happened. As a forklift driver at the Chris Craft warehouse in Trenton, Bobbie had picked up a wooden pallet loaded with boxes and backed out of the warehouse onto a loading dock. He had done this thousands of times over the past eleven years. Turning his head, he saw a tractor-trailer with its rear doors open and its side panel painted with a yellow Criterian Motor Freight logo. Its loading bed was flush with the loading dock. After slowly turning the forklift around, he revved the engine and pulled a lever that raised the forks. He pushed the gas pedal again, shifted into gear and the forklift crawled forward until its front wheels hit the steel edge of the dock. He heard the rumbling sound of the wheels hitting the metal floor of the trailer.

But the trailer began moving away from the dock. As the gap between trailer and dock widened, Bobbie's rear wheels couldn't make it to the trailer. Forklift and Bobbie crashed to the concrete four feet below, leaving him with a broken leg, broken hip bones and part of his spine ripped apart.

I told Roann I would help her, anticipating that I would refer the case to an experienced personal injury lawyer and receive a fee if the case was won.

The next day, I sat in a chair in front of a desk cluttered with files in the office of a bald man with a handlebar mustache. I wanted the Trenton lawyer who "got the big settlements" to help Bobbie. He told me how difficult it would be to win Bobbie's case and how expensive it would be to take a chance on it. Experts had to be hired and paid for their investigation and testimony. Bobbie's doctors wouldn't testify without being paid handsome sums. Bobbie and Roann didn't need help with medical bills, he said, because Bobby had nothing, so the doctors wouldn't sue him.

Bobbie's injury case appeared to be a big one. I didn't want to be like my waiting room buddies' lawyers. I told my father what had happened to Bobbie and with Mr. Mustache. He suggested I go to the Chris Craft warehouse to get a first-hand look at what Bobbie had told me about and then go to another lawyer, who with more information might take on Bobbie's cause. Maybe if I walked a mile in Bobbie's shoes at Chris Craft I would be in a better position to present his case?

I spotted a sign for the Chris Craft warehouse. I had never been on a loading dock at a warehouse, nor had I ever operated a forklift or driven a tractor-trailer. To see for myself what Bobbie was talking about, I turned toward the warehouse. Tractors and trailers were entering the loading area, stopping and backing up to a raised concrete platform edged with a thick steel plate. Every time a tractor-trailer stopped, a loud whoosh escaped. The driver walked to the bottom of the loading dock, picked up a couple of triangular wooden blocks and put them down in front of the vehicle's front wheels. Then he placed two more wooden blocks in front of the rear wheels.

The drivers climbed a set of stairs at one end of the platform, walked over to their trailers, opened the rear doors and walked through a door to the warehouse. Forklift trucks with loads on the forks came out onto the loading dock, were driven into the trailers, set their loads down, backed out and returned to the warehouse. Truck drivers came out of the warehouse, closed the doors to the trailer, descended the stairs, removed the wooden blocks, put them at the base of the loading dock and drove away.

I visited another personal injury lawyer, who told me what Mr. Mustache had said. I went to see Mr. Mustache again. He wouldn't take the case. His waxed ends jiggled up and down when I told him I was going to handle Bobbie's case myself. He guffawed, "If you're going to be a jackass, you ought to go to my good friend Bill Bischoff's seminar. He is talking this weekend." I took the advice.

Bischoff's message in the one-day seminar was "With preparation you can stand up to the most experienced trial lawyer. Be yourself. Show the jury you believe in your case, how much work you put into your case, and tell them stories that will make them identify with your client's cause. That's been my formula."

While Bobbie remained in the hospital for six weeks, unable to bend his knees and ankles, with shooting pains in his legs, I prepared. I witnessed that he couldn't sit or walk and was moody and depressed. After he was transferred to a rehabilitation facility, I watched therapists teach him how to bend and lift his leg and to walk again. I cheered him up just as I had Ellen when she was depressed about her injuries.

Medical reports from his orthopedist, neurologist, and physical therapist included terms such as lumbar, vertebrae, fibromyositis, Harrington rods, compression fracture, Steinman pins, and tibia and fibula, all new to me, so I read books about orthopedics, studying the bone structure of the back and legs. I learned there was more to a broken bone than a crack, that damaged nerves also caused pain, that surgically installed Harrington rods prevented the spine from bending normally, and that bone deformities irritated muscles surrounding the spine. In the years to come, dedicated doctors, nurses and caregivers like Bobbie's taught me medicine.

Wondering how a trailer could move away from the loading dock if its air brakes were set, I called an experienced trial lawyer, who suggested I contact Professor Richard Wolf, who taught a course at the Newark College of Engineering to students heading toward a career in the air brake industry. Wolf looked like a tackle on a college football team. "You want to learn about air brakes, do you? Tell me about your case." I gave him one detail after another.

Wolf picked up a piece of black garden hose from a table. "See this hose I have in my hand? I'm going to put my finger in one end. You blow into the hose." Wolf leaned over and put the hose up to my mouth. "Now blow." I puckered my lips and exhaled. "Keep blowing. Now put your thumb in the other end and stop blowing." I followed his instructions.

We were standing about a foot apart, his finger in one end of the tube and my thumb in the other.

"Do you think the hose is completely filled with air?"

"Sure," I said feeling foolish and wanting to dispel embarrassment from not knowing something that seemed so elementary.

"You're right. The hose is completely full. But there's an element of pressure. Pressure's important. When you took your mouth off of the hose some of the air that you blew in escaped, causing the air pressure to go down."

He explained that when a tractor driver pulls a lever, a compressor pushes air into hoses and as he releases the lever, air escapes. When the truck is running, the air heats up, so the pressure goes up. But when a truck is not running, the air cools and the pressure is reduced even more. The truck wasn't running when Bobbie ran his forklift into it, so the air brake wouldn't have enough pressure to prevent the trailer from rolling a foot or two away from the loading dock if a heavy forklift moved forward into it. Because air brakes have some give to them unless the motor is running, the driver has to use chocks, wooden blocks pointed at one end, to prevent the rig from rolling.

Wolf believed the insurance company and its lawyer would use the air brakes to confuse me, but the issue was as simple as trying to tie a balloon without losing any air, which is impossible. "Hire me to be your expert witness. I'm a hundred an hour and I need three days' notice to testify," he offered, smiling.

In his seminar, Bill Bischoff had taken off one of his shoes and limped around the room as he lectured. Did he have a shoe that was too tight? A few minutes later, he stopped and talked about a client who had a leg one inch shorter than the other. He had urged the jury to take off one of their shoes in the jury room so they could feel what his client experienced every time he took a step. Bischoff urged his audience to let the injured client describe how their injury affected them because "a lawyer has to be able to put the jury in the client's shoes."

How could I do that for Bobbie? I asked him to tell me about his injuries in a way that a third grader would understand. "I'm like Humpty Dumpty who the doctors tried to put back together again." "I want to work like I used to," made me think about "The Little Engine that Could" that I read to Jared. Bobbie was a "Little Engine that Couldn't," but wished he could. He compared himself to Little Jack Horner who sat in the corner.

When the day of the trial came a year later, Bobbie limped to the witness stand and gingerly took his seat. He looked at each juror, following my instructions to talk to the jurors after I asked him a question. My questions and his answers taught the jury how to operate a forklift. He described how the trailer rolled away from the loading dock as he entered it. He described his injuries, his disability, his financial difficulties because he earned much less than he did when he operated a forklift and the resulting depression.

Bobbie's wife, his doctors, and Professor Wolf testified. The defense put its witnesses on the stand.

Eight days after the trial began, five courthouse junkies, who made a life out of going from courtroom to courtroom watching trials and waiting for verdicts, waited with me for the jury to return. Two hours had passed slowly when one of the double courtroom doors opened. A Sheriff's Officer waving an envelope poked his head in. I broke out in a cold sweat. The defense lawyer looked at me, smiled and turned to the Sheriff's Officer. "Bring them in," he said confidently.

Judge Leonard took the Bench. Twelve jurors, ten men and two women, stood expressionless in front of their seats. The first juror opened an envelope and took out a piece of paper. I closed my eyes. "We find in favor of Robert McKenzie against Criterian Motor Freight in the sum of one hundred and fifty thousand dollars."

When I opened my eyes, Judge Leonard spun around in his chair. The

Sheriff's Officer looked at the defense lawyer, who shrugged his shoulders in disbelief.

It was the first six-figure verdict in Trenton's legal history. A jury had put a value on Bobbie's life.

The thrill of winning a case for a person who was unable to afford a lawyer and who had put his blind faith in me was indescribable. Never had I imagined that getting money for someone could be so rewarding.

Three months after Bobbie and Roann received their money, they called me to celebrate. At dinner, he told my father and me that he was going to buy a big boat and spend the rest of his life fishing. My father suggested that Bobbie see a vocational counselor and a financial advisor. Bobbie learned that he needed to be with people to be happy and that couldn't do heavy labor anymore. Roann liked to cook.

With the help of the financial advisor and a realtor, Bobbie bought a tavern in a working class section of Trenton near the Chris Craft warehouse. A few months later, I parked in front of a spanking new neon sign flashing the name THE RED FOX—the nickname of the defense lawyer.

Bobbie built a successful business, working at something that did not require hard labor like running a forklift. His Chris Craft buddies became his customers and they brought their buddies to enjoy Bobbie's gift of gab and Roann's food. Bobbie did okay. He was able to buy the fishing boat he wanted so much.

After Bobbie passed away, his children presented me with a glassed wooden case, which hung on a wall in Bobbie's boat. In it was a clock and barometer. On the case was a brass plaque inscribed with the words "In honor of many years of cherished friendship." Captain Bobbie's clock and barometer hangs on the office wall behind my desk.

I fought one battle after another for people like Bobbie who did not have the ability to fight anger, revenge, and financial destruction themselves. They were in an unfamiliar place in the midst of unfamiliar people. They were different people who they did not know and who their family, close relatives and friends did not know. What they had been was dead. They were different, even though they were literally alive.

Talented engineering professionals like Professor Wolf taught me engineering principles and accident reconstruction. Finding a way to win and a pocket deep enough to pay for the harm caused was too often elusive, but when you made it happen, it felt wonderful to be able to add quality to a life.

I learned that it was the job of defense lawyers to prevent people from collecting money and that to successfully deal with them I needed to display a tough exterior. Like a doctor, I could not fall apart at the sight of a life being maimed. I couldn't go home and beat my head on the bathtub when a defense lawyer had me on the ropes.

Rebuilding cities. That dream faded. In case after case, I experienced gratification from helping people whose lives were changed in a millisecond because someone else was careless. In order not to be the kind of lawyer my waiting room buddies disliked, I assembled a team of lawyers and legal assistants to provide the services that seriously injured people and their families needed. David Botwinick, Eric Ludwig, John Sakson, Robert Bratman, Chris Pyne, Bruce Stern, Paul Daly and David Cohen formed the core of the Stark and Stark legal team. Nancy Karlosky, my secretary, became the team captain. Florance Churchill, Mary Ann Papp, Lisa Williams, Debby Toth, Michele Greenwood, Lynn McDonald and Kathy Farrell served as legal assistants who provided technical, investigative and social support to our clients and us. Over the years, Stark and Stark developed specialty teams for brain, spinal cord and burn injuries, as well as construction and nursing home accidents.

Unfortunately, during my career, people who were not as lucky as Bobbie— and me—called, complaining that they had settled for too little money because the ambulance chaser was only out for his one-third. Some had lost their case and now wanted a "second opinion" after they had gone to the lawyer who had drafted their will or handled the closing when they bought a house. Too many had responded to a slick television advertisement promising fast cash. Others had become victims twice because they didn't know how to ask the right questions.

My experience showed me that seriously injured didn't have to be unlucky. There are a cadre of excellent lawyers, experts in the representation of seriously injured persons. Seriously injured people have the right to the best and most qualified lawyer to represent them, no matter what their social, educational or economic background. Contingent fee agreements are available everywhere in United States.

I have read books about the brain, the spinal cord and burns. I have attended and taught seminars. But there is no book or seminar about what a seriously injured person has to do to navigate the legal system or a book about what happens after the case is over.

In 2002, I wrote Beyond the Bar—Challenges in a Lawyer's Life—a book about my experiences during the first fifteen years of my lawyer life, a book that showed how the challenges I faced shaped me as a person and lawyer.

I thought about what I needed to do to complete my career, to give meaning and purpose to a life in court, to have something beyond the rush of a seven figure verdict, the celebratory dinner, the thank you letter, the pat on the back.

That's when Nina Rich called. Nina is the mother of a boy so severely brain injured in an automobile crash that he has been institutionalized for twenty-two years. Although Terry Rich was awarded sufficient funds to afford the finest care available for the rest of his life, Nina had called me more times than I can count for help and advice.

Now, on August 26, 2008, she was angry. She had just read the New York Times story about Staff Sergeant Kevin Owley, an Iraq War veteran struggling to unscramble his memory and thoughts, getting lost on the road, even with directions, and writing his appointments down but still forgetting a few. The article said that little is known medically by doctors or scientists about what happens to a brain as a result of powerful bomb blasts as opposed to car crashes on a highway, blows to the head on a football field or a bullet wound.

"This government of ours sends boys to Iraq and Afghanistan," she said. "They buy the best bombers and missiles and then one of our boys gets hit. They get the best medical care in field hospitals and rehabilitation centers, but after that, guess what? They're not lucky. They get dumped! Some commander-in-chief we have. He never provided for long-term care facilities to take care of our heroes. Worse yet, there's a shortage of adequate facilities for those who can pay for them."

I hung up thinking about how in 2008, at least a million people—civilians injured in accidents and soldiers returning from Afghanistan and Iraq—faced challenges presented by a catastrophic injury. Why not try to write the book about what it took to survive courtroom drama, to advocate for the seriously injured people? Why not share the stories of my clients—courtroom warriors—with our brave soldiers who came back suffering from serious injuries?

I read a book, Head Cases, written by Michael Paul Mason, a caseworker who helped people like those I fought for in court and afterward. He answered many questions. But not those asked by my rehabilitation buddies.

To tell the rest of the story, I called Angelo, and Linda, Josh, Andy, and Skylar and others like them. I oftentimes lost touch with them after the case was over except at times when they needed help. Sometimes I was frustrated that a chasm separated me from those who I had fought for and lost sleep over. Other times, I thought it was a blessing that they were out of my mind and that I could concentrate on the cases on my plate. I learned that people either didn't want to bother me or didn't want to think of me because I brought back memories that they wanted to bury.

When I told them what I wanted to do, they were happy. They wanted to help others. They met with me and analyzed what they went through on the way to court and what happened to them after the case was over. We talked about what we did right and discussed what we would have done differently, hindsight being 20-20.

They showed me that there is a disconnect between those who are suffering and the rest of the world. They had not understood the obstacles they faced in their quest for justice and neither did the public, who looks at large settlements that people receive and assumes that they are set for the rest of their lives. That is wrong. Considering the cost of treatment for a severe injury, even one million dollars, invested prudently, may barely cover expenses.

My work had not blinded me to the fact that a big verdict doesn't fix a seriously injured person's life. For some people, the money really helps, providing the opportunity for a high quality of life. For others, the money does not help at all, and can even make things worse by raising their expectations to unrealistic levels. But my eyes have been opened to the stark reality that not winning a verdict or a settlement likely leads to a life of squalor in an institutional warehouse with an abominable quality of life.

I interviewed doctors, who under the most trying conditions, put people back together again and rehabilitation professionals, who helped people regain mobility and learn to speak again, and caregivers who ameliorated indescribable suffering. They saw serious injury from their perspective.

Mine was different. I often arrived on the heels of the catastrophe, shepherding the flock through an emotional medical and legal maze, and staying with the injured person and their families for years afterward.

Limited in their actions and abilities, sometimes confined to institutions or their homes, it is easy to see seriously injured people as non-human and dismiss or look away from them. People with serious injuries live unimaginably trying lives. They may not be able to stand, to walk, to recall memories or think consciously. They may not even be able to read or write or speak.

I wrote this book to help seriously injured people survive the heat and drama of the courtroom and life beyond the verdict. I wrote to plead with the public to give seriously injured people a voice so that the value of their lives are not forgotten. I wrote to bring to life what it is like to advocate for the seriously injured.

The Take Away section that follows the stories teach applicable lessons that help the injured person, his or her family and loved ones navigate the voyage from hope to reality.

1. THE LUCKY ONE

Muscular arms hung from twenty-three year old Angelo Angarone's broad shoulders. His hands squeezed the grips on the high bars on his Harley, his eyes dancing as he revved the unmuffied engine like Peter Fonda playing Captain America in Easy Rider. His lifetime friend, Peter, grabbed the sides of the motorcycle seat.

They were three blocks away from the Allstate Seat Covering Shop on South Broad Street in Trenton, New Jersey, headed back to the Allstate parking lot, where, the plan was, Peter would slide off the seat and get into the car in which he had brought Angelo from Clarksburg, twelve miles away, to Allstate to pick up his bike. Angelo would ride the bike home, take off his white T-shirt, jeans and sneakers and don his Shoprite uniform and go to work loading groceries on shelves.

Angelo had brought his motorcycle to the Shop because the foam on the seat had become soft after two years of use and the bump between him and his passenger had flattened, causing the passenger to slide into him as he slowed to a stop. Allstate agreed to redo the seat so that it was, they said, like new. Angelo paid the bill. Peter had suggested they take the bike for a spin.

Angelo lifted his T-shirt and wiped sweat from his forehead. As the light turned green, Angelo's loud take-off caught the attention of a woman standing on the corner. Seconds later, as a blue Chevy turned left suddenly in front of the Harley, she screamed, "Oh my God."

Representing indigent defendants who faced the noose of criminal justice for free was an obligation of New Jersey lawyers. In 1974, I received an assignment—defending a young man charged with urinating in front of a bar on a Trenton street while under the influence of alcohol. Angelo Angarone was a lanky young man wearing a ponytail, his jet-black hair framing an oval face, taller than broad, with deep-set eyes and a prominent nose. His complexion, pale and wan, bespoke a hard life. He admitted to urinating on the street, but adamantly denied he was under the influence of alcohol. "I was in the bar, but didn't drink. I was high on amphetamines. You can't drink when you are drugged up," Angelo said, matter of factly, sitting in the client chair in my office.

A week later, we ambled down Chancery Lane, a cobblestone street, to Judge

Albert Cooper's court. At eight o'clock in the morning, the entrance foyer was crowded, smoky and reeking of alcohol. Angelo, wearing freshly pressed pants, a white shirt and sports jacket, slid onto an oak bench, which was filled with men in blue jeans and plaid shirts and women wearing tight skirts and ballerina shoes. I sidled into a parade of suits carrying brief cases making its way toward a portly police officer.

Dinky Dooling inquired, "How do you plead?"

"Not guilty."

Dinky scanned the summons, setting forth Angelo's crime. "Not guilty?" His Adams apple rolled in his throat.

"Pissing, yes. Intoxication, no." I replied.

Court was scheduled to begin at eight-thirty. The clock was about to strike nine when a tall, imposing man in a black robe introduced himself to the standing room only crowd. "My name is Judge Albert Cooper," he said, gently. "For most people, a court like this is the only one they will see in a lifetime. Here, you can have a lawyer. But you don't need one. If you are guilty, just tell my clerk you are guilty. I'll be more lenient than if you don't tell me the truth. Anyone can make a mistake. I want you to understand one thing. I do not tolerate dishonesty."

Judge Cooper stood. "I will be back in a few minutes. Anyone who wants to plead guilty, see the police officer over there," he said, pointing to the portly blue shirt.

The courtroom was abuzz. A line of guilties formed.

Half an hour later, a door opened and two men, vagrants in appearance entered, escorted by two blue shirts, who seated them in the front row, next to the suits, of which I was one.

"Order in the Court," Dinky barked. "The Municipal Court of Trenton in now in session."

"Good morning, again, Judge Cooper said before calling out, "State versus Melvin David." A policeman ushered Mr. David toward the bench, and pulled his hands behind his back. "Hello, Melvin," Cooper began. "I told you last year that if I ever saw you here again you were going to the workhouse. Right, Melvin?"

"Oh yes, your Honor."

"Then why did Officer Dooling find you last night sleeping outside this courtroom?"

"I got nowhere else to go, Judge. It be getting cold outside. I need my hooch to keep warm."

Melvin was sentenced to six months in the workhouse. Next came Isaac. And then the parade of suits with brief cases followed with their guilty clients. One after another. Forty of them. Then the jeans and tight skirts.

It was now eleven o'clock in the morning, and one case was left. A 'not guilty.' State versus Angarone.

"Do you realize, Mr. Angarone, that if I find you guilty, I will not be lenient like I was with the others?"

Angelo turned toward me, shrugging his shoulders.

"Your Honor, It is the burden of the state to prove all elements of the crime."

"Mr. Dooling, call the witnesses."

"Witnesses in State versus Angarone."

No one answered.

"They were here earlier, your Honor," Dooling said. "They must have become impatient and left."

"No witnesses? Case dismissed," Cooper said. "Mr. Angarone, you are a lucky boy. If the witnesses were here, your case would not have a happy ending. Your nice clothes don't hide your eyes and face. They tell me that something bad is going on with you. My advice. Get your act together or you'll be back here again. Next time, you won't be so lucky."

Angelo and I turned our backs on the courtroom with its barred windows and peeling paint on plaster walls. A limp, sweaty hand thanked me.

It was autumn 1979 when Angelo Angarone's girl friend called me to say he had been in a bad accident, was in the hospital and wanted me to come see him. "He doesn't know if you will remember him," Tracy said. "You helped him out with a drug case." I remembered him.

Tracy and Peter were in Angelo's hospital room. Her tanned round face was topped by hair cut in a fringe, framing high prominent cheekbones. Her eyes were a remarkable gray. Peter's dirty blond hair was pulled back, his hazel eyes full of warmth. Angelo lay in a hospital bed with a trapeze hanging above his head. A beard covered the oval face and the dimples that I remembered. A hand reached out to me. "I can move my arms," he said. He looked down at his toes. "They don't move," he said. "Motorcycle crash."

Drugs, I thought.

"I know what you're thinking," Angelo said. "I've been clean for three years. Did rehab. Ain't that so." His eyes floated to Tracy, who nodded.

"So what happened?"

"We got left-turned," Peter said. "Our way was blocked. Ang dumped the bike, but we still hit the car. There wasn't a big crash. But the sudden stop sent me crashing into Ang's back. I sheared his back with my belt buckle." Peter fingered a Wells Fargo metal buckle.

"I felt the pain in my back. Then I realized I couldn't move. They brought me here."

"You have a good case against the person who left turned you."

Tracy had already had three accident lawyers come to the hospital. They all said the same thing. The old lady driving the Chevy had a $15,000 insurance policy. She doesn't even own a house.

"They told me I don't need a lawyer because her insurance company will pay me the fifteen." Angelo peered at me.

Professor Richard Wolf at the Newark College of Engineering had helped me understand how air brakes worked in Bobbie McKenzie's case. Now he sat behind a cluttered desk.

"So what do we have this time?" he asked.

I told him about pathetic Angelo Angarone. Wolf rolled his eyes. "Low impact. Seat repair." He paused. "There's a colleague on the faculty who designs seats for cars, airplanes, and, I think, motorcycles. Howard Gage."

The renowned engineer who had designed motorcycle seats inspected Angelo's motorcycle in Tracy's garage. Tracy's house was in a dog patch neighborhood, where the front yards were bare or overgrown, driveways filled with junk cars. Tracy lived with an older sister, who was an alcoholic, and an infirm mother.

"The bike has no sliding damage," Gage said. "The bike laid down only after the impact. The impact was slight. Not a lot of speed. Probably close to stopping." Gage patted the seat. "This is a banana seat." Punching the bump, he added, 'The bump is designed to reduce impact between a passenger and a driver, even in low impact collisions. The bump prevents someone seated behind the driver from sliding, as if on a sliding board into the driver's spine." Gage pushed the bump. "It's too soft." He took a penknife from his pocket and made a slit in the new cover. "The bump is old foam," he said, calling Angelo's seat a 'back breaker,' because Allstate used the old worn foam and had rebuilt the bump with tired foam."

"It was supposed to be like new," Angelo had told me. "Even the receipt said it was new foam."

Gage thought we might have a case against the seat upholsterer.

When I suggested Angelo use the $15,000 he would get from the blue Chevy to hire Gage as an expert to testify in court against Allstate, he said, "It's worth a shot."

I met with doctors who showed me X-rays of Angelo's crushed spine. Needle test graphs proved that sensation was gone over the whole surface of Angelo's legs and over his buttocks. I learned how someone lost the use of both legs: the human body is composed of bones—the skeleton—to which are attached a large number of muscles, called voluntary muscles, which possess the ability to contract or relax in response to certain stimuli, which are conveyed to the muscles by means of nerves. The involuntary muscles not under Angelo's control were not working, causing Angelo to lose control of his bladder, lower bowel and sexual organs.

He had to be turned over every two hours day and night so bedsores did not develop. A physiotherapist showed me how he stretched Angelo to prevent stiffness or contractures in the paralyzed limbs and how great care had to be taken for the rest of Angelo's life to prevent urinary infections, which could prove fatal. An occupational therapist, who helped Angelo overcome apathy and depression, explained the importance of counseling about domestic affairs, personal and financial. A speech therapist described how Angelo's brain had been hurt so that he had to make notes to remind himself to do simple tasks because he would forget minutes after he was told what to do.

Paralysis entered my life in 1967 when my wife, Ellen, gave birth to our son. Nine pounds-fourteen ounces, my son's delivery left him without use of his right arm and my wife with paralysis in her right leg. Fourteen months of patterning, visits to a world-famous doctor in New York and a miracle led to their regaining almost full function. I had read many books on neurology. Now I had to learn about paralysis that would never go away. But there was only one book, a study of paraplegia in England written by J.J. Walsh, available in 1979. I read it over and over, seeking answers to questions I had about Angelo's physical and mental condition and the treatment he was getting.

While I tried cases, interviewed new clients, and my wife and two children demanded more and more of my time, I was getting to know Angelo and Tracy. How long would Tracy stay with Angelo? Doctors told me that Angelo's injuries prevented him from ever getting an erection. I didn't think it would be too long before a twenty-two year old girl would strike out for greener pastures. One day, I came out with it. "How are you guys doing with sex?"

Angelo's lips turned up at the ends. Tracy's neck flushed red. Angelo stuck out his tongue, wagging it like a dog and fisted his hand, except for his middle finger. "I take good care of you, don't I?"

Angelo had been released from the hospital, just shy of six months after the collision. From then onward, Tracy was at his side, turning him so that he did not develop bedsores, catheterizing him so that he did not develop urinary infections, examining his buttocks to discover redness that could lead to infection. She was all he had. His mother and father were distant. "He's always been too much to handle," his mother told me once when I asked if he could move back home if Tracy ever deserted him.

Three long years later, Angelo sat beside me in an empty courtroom—a lonely place—its windows draped with heavy gold damask. Portraits of judges, omnisciently peering out, hung on the walnut paneled walls. A bronze statue of a blindfolded woman stood on a table next to the judge's bench, a sword in her right hand and a balance scale in her left. Her foot crushed a deadly snake against a book of the law, the cornerstone upon which all of society rested. She had a tranquil smile. But I felt uneasy.

After Peter, doctors, nurses, therapists, Tracy and Angelo had testified, describing Angelo's life and his future, Howard Gage settled in the witness box. He had grey hair, cut short, and he wore frameless glasses. His salt and pepper beard made him appear older than a man in his forties. Gage had built a scale model of the Harley, the seat, and the positions of Angelo and Peter at the moment of impact. Two lawyers from my office carried the model into the courtroom and placed it in front of the witness box. After telling the jury what he did investigating the case, explaining how his educational background and experience made him an expert, qualified to testify in court, he demonstrated that Peter's belt buckle struck Angelo in the exact location where the spine had been crushed, severing his spinal cord. Then Gage showed how a firm bump on the seat would have lessened the impact enough to prevent that.

Vincent Sponziello, the owner of Allstate Seat Cover Shop, had grey hair, straight and a touch unruly brushed over a high forehead. As he testified in a deep voice, he gave the impression that he was confident and secure. He told the jury that the old foam, while soft, was built up so that the bump was even higher than on the original banana seat.

During cross-examination, I showed Mr. Sponziello the receipt he gave

Angelo Angarone when he picked up his motorcycle on August 25, 1979.

"Beneath the words, Allstate Seat Cover Shop, are there other words?"

"Yes." He raised his chin and furrowed bushy brows, a touch of arrogance, so I thought. "Please read them to the jury."

Sponziello's eyes twitched. He fumbled with the receipt. His lips rubbed together. "Expert Reuphosterer. Seats Recovered. Like New."

Asking one question too many to an opposing witness is dangerous, especially if you don't know the answer. Turning to Sponziello, I eyed the jury. It was a sea of blank expressions. Sponziello pushed himself up from the witness chair. "One more question, sir." He sunk politely. "Mr. Sponziello, would you tell the jury what it would have cost you to have used new foam for Mr. Angarone's banana seat bump?"

"About four dollars."

"No further questions." My jaw tightened, I wheeled around and shook my head from side to side.

Allstate Seat Cover Shop's lawyer railed in his summation, pointing at Angelo and me. 'Suing a motorcycle seat. Are they out of their minds? A motorcycle seat caused someone to become a paraplegic? Get real!" he bellowed before blaming Angelo's tragedy on the driver of the blue Chevy.

The lawyer for the blue Chevy admitted his client's guilt, telling the jury that it was up to Angelo's lawyer to convince them that Allstate Seat Cover Shop was responsible.

I had gone to my high school and borrowed hurdles used in track meets. During my summation, I placed two hurdles in front of the jury box, illustrating the hurdles that Angelo had jumped over and those that he would never scale. I hoped I was dramatizing the jumps Angelo had to make to overcome fainting when he sat up, regaining the power of balancing by using his eyes to tell him how and when he was changing position, and to develop the non-paralyzed muscles of his arms and upper trunk to take over some of the duties of the paralyzed muscles.

I approached the jurors. "But for four dollars we wouldn't be here today." Leaning stiff-armed on the jury rail, I pled, "Angelo's case is important to him but also to others. A verdict against Allstate Seat Cover Shop is a verdict for the consumer, a verdict that will speak loudly, and a verdict that will tell businesses to do what they were asked to do or face consequences. A verdict for Angelo is a verdict for safety."

Six hours of waiting in an empty courtroom ended when a door to the left of the jury box opened and a Sheriff's Officer dressed in a yellow shirt and brown pants with a yellow stripe delivered the long-waited announcement, "We have a verdict."

I had tried to introduce jurors to Angelo's world. Had I shown them what it was like to live sitting down and unable to remember what happened just minutes ago? Had the jury appreciated Angelo's hard work using parallel bars in front of a large mirror or learning to use a monkey pole over his bed so that someone could adjust pillows under his buttocks and legs?

What were three of the twelve jurors thinking when they leaned forward as Angelo described the difficulty he had doing things they took for granted, like moving one's bowels by inserting suppositories or urinating through a catheter? What was going through the mind of the juror with his arms across his chest and pursed lips or the two who were expressionless? Until I met Angelo, I had shunned people who were disabled, those who sat in wheelchairs or who were deformed, afraid to think about what their lives were like, fearing and thinking that 'there but for the Grace of God goes I.'

The judge emerged from a door behind the bench.

"All rise," the Sheriff's Officer bellowed.

Oh my God, I thought. Here we were at the moment of truth. No doubt Angelo would receive a verdict against the blue Chevy, but fifteen thousand dollars would not cover the money I had invested in the case. I had spent $50,000 for doctors' testimony and Howard Gage's services, model and testimony. If he could pay $5000 in medical bills not paid by Shoprite's insurance company, and close to $50,000 after paying me back and my fee of one-third, Angelo would be happy. The Allstate insurance lawyer offered us $50,000, "not a dime more." Angelo and I had no choice but to take a chance.

Tracy, who had stuck with Angelo, despite knowing how difficult his future would be, sat with her eyes closed. I had convinced Angelo's mother and father to attend the trial so that the jury would see a family that was concerned about him. Angelo's father and mother had not been in his life after he had become addicted to drugs and had impregnated a woman twice. They steepled their hands in prayer.

The lawyer for the blue car rocked on his heels. His client had no assets. He had nothing to lose.

Seated in the wheelchair to which he had been sentenced moments after the crash, Angelo grabbed my hand.

The jury foreman fingered a piece of paper.

The lawyer representing Allstate Seat Cover Shop nonchalantly twirled his glasses in his fingers. Even though, under New Jersey law in 1979, I only had to prove that the Allstate Seat Cover Shop was 1% negligent in order to collect an entire verdict from Allstate, three veteran trail lawyers had refused his case. Was that why he was so confident?

To disguise my nervousness, I fingered the yellowed pages of Understanding Paraplegia, by J.J. Walsh, a book that I had read over and over while learning about Angelo's life and his future. Now, I could not restrain myself. I glanced at the jury. Juror #3 smiled at me. My heart skipped a beat. The other eleven jurors? Poker faces all.

The judge read a question. "Were Angelo Angarone's injuries caused by the driver of the blue Chevy?" *"Yes."*

I closed my eyes, afraid to hear the answer to the next question.

"Were Angelo Angarone's injuries caused by Allstate Seat Cover Shop?" The jury foreman answered, *"Yes."* and I felt Angelo's hand grip my wrist.

"In what percentage?"

"The blue Chevy – 50%"

"Allstate Seat Cover Shop – 50%"

"What amount will fairly compensate Angelo?"

"$3,500,000."

I had never seen Angelo cry—not after his doctor told him he would never walk again, not when Tracy catheterized him. Not when a drug store step became an insurmountable barrier. Now, tears streamed down Angelo's cheeks. I had made up my mind to be expressionless, expecting the worse.

Whoopee went round and round in my head.

A newspaper reporter approached Angelo as he wheeled out of the courthouse. "What do you think about the verdict?"

"Today is a great day for the consumer," Angelo replied, smiling broadly.

The next day, a banner headline in a Trenton paper read, *MAN AWARDED RECORD DAMAGES FROM SUIT. 3.5M AWARD.*

"The largest amount ever awarded by a jury in Central Jersey and possibly the entire state," court personnel were quoted as saying. And Angelo had told the reporter, "Mentally I couldn't handle it. It's a good thing I was heavily sedated with morphine at the time. I was just hoping for enough to pay my bills. Those bills total $5,000."

I didn't know it then that the article would provoke such unpopularity. Many asked me, "Why so much money?" Many, including Kevin Quinn, a fellow member of the Junior Chamber of Commerce, called me "Stark the Shark" and criticized me, complaining that I was putting a hardworking businessman out of business and that insurance premiums would go up. I had taken on a case, at great risk, to help someone and was derided for my efforts.

It didn't take long for Angelo to blow my mind. In my office, he waved a $2,200,000 check, exclaiming, "I hit the lottery."

I worried.

A month later, he wheeled into my office and, with a smile from ear to ear, asked, "How do you like my new racing wheelchair?" My Adams apple rolled in my neck. "You're looking at the next Para-Olympic gold medal winner," he said. Two weeks later he rented a garage and began building a three-wheeled motorcycle. Then he hired a stockbroker who was going to make him "very rich."

When Nancy, my secretary, told me, "Angelo is on the telephone," I cringed, afraid to hear what was coming next.

Angelo's spinal surgeon had opened my eyes to the mental processes paralyzed persons go through, by explaining that paraplegics faced enormous risks of infection often leading to an early death. The "live and let live" syndrome was, he said, "natural." Angelo had rationalized that he could die any day so why not spend and live for today.

After the case was over there was a disruption of his relationship with Peter, who stopped coming to see him. I called Peter, who had been an impressive witness at the trial. I listened to Peter tell me, "He's too much to take care of. It's too tough even to go to a movie." I thought about what Peter said and understood it. Or so I thought.

While talking to a psychiatrist about another client, I discussed my conversation with Peter. The psychiatrist told me that Peter probably felt guilty, thinking that he contributed to his friend's injury. Thereafter, when clients were shunned by close friends like Peter I suggested they seek help in allaying their guilt.

Angelo faced a challenge. How could he tell the difference between people he could really trust and people who were just seeing him as a financial opportunity? How did he choose someone to help manage his money so that it would be there when he needed it in the future?

How could I convince Angelo to understand that he needed protection from his own behavior without insulting him or putting down his ability?

With the help of his parents, who were suddenly interested in Angelo's well being, I connected him with a banker experienced with children who had large inheritances. Knowing how to protect heirs from themselves, he convinced Angelo to put a million dollars into an annuity paying enough in interest to provide funds for good medical and home care.

Two years later, Angelo called me. He had spent $5,000 for a penal implant. "Best bucks I ever spent," he railed. He thanked me for directing him to the banker, who had persuaded him to "get out of the stock market which had tanked."

He continued to live at Tracy's where her alcoholic sister and infirm mother preyed upon Angelo's sympathies, wresting close to $10,000 from him before he wised up. As the sister became drunker and drunker, she treated Angelo and her mother roughly. Angelo recalled his problems with drugs and realized that he was pouring money down a drain.

One afternoon, a Trenton policeman called to tell me that, "A client of yours has been riding a scooter down the middle of a heavily traveled street. His name is Angelo."

"Put him on the telephone."

"I just bought a new mobility chair," Angelo explained, "and I'm giving it a test drive. I thought it would be safer to drive on the yellow line—so drivers can see me from both directions."

The policeman agreed to escort Angelo back to the mobility store with wigwags flashing.

On another occasion, a nurse called me. "I have a client of yours here. He has a urinary tract infection. He just asked me for a cigarette and a light. He offered me fifty dollars. It's against hospital regulations."

"So?"

"Fifty dollars is a lot of money."

"So why are you calling me?"

"He said if he ran out of money, he'd just call his lawyer, Albert Stark."

I knew without her telling me who the client was.

The harsh winters in New Jersey were hard on Angelo. He and Tracy relocated to Florida, where they bought a house on a river and for many years I lost touch with them. One day, I spotted an obituary in the paper. Angelo's mother had died. I was curious about what happened to Angelo and Tracy. I found where he lived through a doctor who had treated him. When I asked Angelo why he stopped sending me holiday cards, he replied, "When I think about you, I relive the bad times. I needed to get on with my life. Sure, I appreciated everything you did for me. But..." his voice trailed off.

Tracy became a well-paid physical therapist, working in a rehabilitation hospital. Over the years, Angelo survived infections and depression, thanks to Tracy and his team of doctors. They had learned how to deal with depression, how to deal with people who resented him because they thought he received too much money for a case he did not deserve to win.

Angelo's money enabled him to benefit from many technological advances that over the years made his life easier—mechanized wheelchairs, handicapped ramps and parking spaces, electric stimulators for his legs, and motorized chairs and vans. He still rides the three-wheeled motorcycle he had built. Angelo designed a winch to lift him in his wheelchair from his dock to his speedboat. I received a 2007 Christmas card with a photo on the cover. Angelo and Tracy smiled, sitting in a boat tied up to a dock.

He and Tracy had overcome hurdles many seriously-injured can not jump over. He had learned to look forward without constantly thinking about and being emotionally hamstrung by the past.

2. SKY QUEEN

Kevin Quinn, the same Kevin Quinn who belittled me after I won Angelo Angarone's case, was now an executive at Bell Telephone. He had, along with CNN, MSNBC, and Fox News, been advocating laws limiting peoples' rights, calling them "tort reform," arguing for free markets and individual responsibility. He saw lawyers, especially personal injury lawyers, as a problem because the six and seven figure verdicts they won, to his mind, put companies out of business, chased doctors from the medical practice and caused drug companies to charge higher prices.

Kevin's daughter—Skylar—was a high school senior, one of the best students in her class, headed to a Big Ten university with a scholarship. Elected Senior Prom Queen, she had been a member of the band for four years. Only seven months before, she had been high-stepping in front of the marching band, twirling a baton effortlessly, clad in a purple skirt and a gold vest, her strawberry blonde hair peeking out from beneath a flawless white top hat, the colors of the Holy Spirit High School Saints. The marching band followed her to midfield in Giants Stadium, where she tossed her baton high spinning it once, twice, three times. Just as it was about to hit the turf, Skylar snatched it. Two boys with flaming torches ran up to her and lit both ends of her baton. When the boys lifted her into the air, flaming baton spinning, the packed stands erupted into thunderous approval. The judges announced that Skylar's school had won the New Jersey State Band Championship.

The May weekend trip to Virginia Beach was a reward for the victory. It was early afternoon when the bus dropped the band off at the Surfside International Beach Hotel. Skylar shared a room with two of her closest friends. This would be one of the best trips of her life.

When Kevin got to my office, I learned that Skylar had broken her neck diving into a pool at the hotel. Her condition was too serious for her to be transported back to New Jersey, and the doctors thought she would be paralyzed for life. He told me, John Sakson, a partner in our firm, and Florance Churchill, a legal assistant, that he was worried about medical bills and what he would do when his insurance ran out, especially if she really would be paralyzed for the rest of her life. We all knew from experience that when families of injured people met with a lawyer to discuss medical bills, what they really wanted to know was whether or not they had a legal case.

Skylar's friends, Judy and Claire, had told Kevin that she dove into a pool that had two shallow ends.

"Were there lifeguards?" John asked.

"I don't think so."

"Was there anything wrong with the pool?"

Kevin's brow furrowed. "Judy and Claire mentioned that the water was cloudy."

I had learned that many cases looked hopeless at first glance, but actually were not. Most accidents didn't happen without someone's carelessness.

The next day John, Florance and I checked into the Surfside International Beach Hotel in Virginia Beach and made our way to the pool. There was not much activity—just several hotel guests lounging on pool chairs, working on their tans. The pool itself was tranquil. The water was crystal clear and reflected the rays of the bright sun, shimmering and sloshing idyllically in the slight breeze. With the peaceful scene laid out before our eyes, it was sobering to think that only little more than a week ago a soon-to-be high school graduate with everything to look forward to had lain in the water with a broken neck, her life irrevocably altered in little more than a heartbeat.

"Look at that. Warning signs." Florance was pointing at three large signs beyond the far end of the pool, facing the pool entrance through which we had come and clearly visible to anyone. Each sign consisted of black, capital letters on a white background: "CAUTION: NO LIFEGUARD ON DUTY," one of them said. Another announced, "SWIM AT YOUR OWN RISK." Yet another warned, "NO RUNNING."

"There's no sign that says 'no diving'," I remarked.

"There's no diving board," Florance said, as if to say, so what, you fool.

I walked to an end of the pool and slid in. The water came up to my waist. I paddled toward the other end. The water deepened up to my chest. "3"s were painted in black on the walls inside the pool where I had entered and "5"s where I was standing. There were "3"s clearly visible on the wall at the other end too.

"This is a volleyball pool," John exclaimed.

"What's that?"

"They put a net in the middle and the teams stand on either side. I played in one in Bermuda once."

Why would Skylar dive if she knew the pool was shallow? It was easy to see the bottom. Something didn't fit.

"You think someone pushed Skylar into the pool? Was there horsing around?" John asked.

I toweled off and sat on a lounge chair. Florance shuffled over to a soda vending machine. When she returned, she said, "Aren't there usually numbers painted on the deck of a pool? I didn't see any on my way to the soda machine." The three of us circled the pool. On the far side, there were worn-out remnants of a "3" and a "5" and a "3." The deck where we were sitting was a different color than the deck on the other side and the cement appeared to be new.

John thought that the pool deck had been repaired, but the numbers never repainted and we might have a case after all, but Florance, always the skeptic, remarked. "The numbers on the pool wall are plain as day."

Back in New Jersey, I told Kevin that we couldn't understand why Skylar would dive head first into a section of shallow water that was clearly marked.

"I can't either," he said. "Kids being kids, I thought there might have been some horsing around." Just as John had thought.

"Judy and Claire denied it, and a chaperone that I trust said that nothing like that was happening on the pool deck. What sticks in my mind is that Judy said she could barely see a shadow. They had just opened the pool for the kids. You know how pools are when they first open. The water isn't filtered yet. Maybe that's why Skylar didn't realize how shallow the water was?"

Florance had an idea. "You know what kids do when they go on any school trip? They take pictures! Let's ask around and see if anyone has pictures of the pool."

"I can't do it," Kevin said. "Skylar is still in spinal shock and on a ventilator. Maureen is still with her, and I'm heading back down tomorrow."

"We can write a letter," Florance suggested.

"That will make parents think Kevin and Maureen are out to sue somebody," I said.

Kevin suggested that he and Maureen write the letter. We all agreed and minutes later, we had one:

Dear Band Member,

Thanks to so many of you that have sent cards, balloons, and letters to Skylar. They have cheered her up. Skylar was not able to attend the pool or beach parties during the special weekend. She would love to have mementos and pictures. If you bring us pictures that you took, we will put them together into an album for Skylar.

Skylar's Mom and Dad,

Maureen and Kevin Quinn

Within days, pictures poured in. Pictures of the pool showed the top half of a "3," but the bottom half was obscured by opaque water. When the sun was behind the camera, the top half of the "3" reflected in the water, making it look like an "8". The cloudy, greenish gray water was higher than it had been when we were there. John said that Skylar could easily have mistaken the '3' for an '8.'

"Assuming she even looked at the depth markers," Florance added.

Judy and Claire sat in a living room in the presence of Judy's mother and Claire's father. I explained that what they told me would be important to Skylar.

"We don't want our daughters involved," Judy's mother said.

"I don't know what the girls will tell me, whether they will be involved, whether there is anything I can do for Skylar. If Judy was in the predicament Skylar is in, I am sure you would want Skylar to help."

Judy's mother eyed Claire's father.

"You're not going to record or take notes of what they say."

"Not if you don't want me to."

"I guess it's okay, then," Judy's mother said.

"Let's start with when you got to your room," I said to Judy.

"We put our bathing suits on and went out. Some kids went to the beach, others stayed at the pool. Skylar forgot her goggles and went back for them and when she came back, Claire and I were standing in water up to our waist. Skylar walked over to us and dipped her foot into the water. 'It's cold,'" she said.

"The water wasn't so bad once you got in," Claire added.

Skylar had circled the pool to the deep end. She walked over to the edge. She dipped her foot in the water again. She positioned her hands over her head and crouched down low, and then her legs uncoiled and propelled her high into the air. She hung there for a moment, and then flew headfirst into the water.

Judy and Claire waited for her to come back up. They thought maybe she was holding her breath under the water. Maybe swimming the length of the pool underwater. They got out of the pool and walked toward the deep end. Judy saw a shadow and jumped in. A chill ran up her spine as her feet made contact with the tiled floor, the water only up to her waist.

Judy flailed her arms, trying to find Skylar, finally grabbing hold of an arm.

Judy's piercing yell quieted everyone. Claire took Skylar's arm and Judy pushed. Skylar's eyes were closed and her head tilted at an awkward angle. A chaperone ran to a red telephone and called 911.

From cases that I had handled outside of New Jersey, I knew that different jurisdictions had different laws and it was important to hire local lawyers. Defense attorneys filed motions, forcing an out-of-state lawyer to make multiple trips back and forth, and judges often "home-towned" out-of-state lawyers by postponing hearing dates and trials, making things more difficult than they should be. So I went to see Richard Reynolds in downtown Norfolk, Virginia, who I knew from trial lawyers' conventions. Reynolds had a reputation for securing multimillion-dollar verdicts and settlements.

He was short, with jet-black hair and a thick goatee, and wore a black suit with a white shirt and a striped red tie. A crystal chandelier hung above his oversized walnut desk. I described what I had learned about Skylar's accident, spreading the band members' pictures on his desk. "Looks like the bottom of the pool and the depth markings are obscured by the murkiness and height of the water," he said. "That's negligence. Improper maintenance." He lifted a picture. "No markings on the pool deck. That's a bummer. Negligence for sure."

I pulled out a one-inch thick pamphlet, the standards established by the American National Standards Institute to define product safety. The ANSI standards for commercial swimming pools required depth markings on both the sides of a pool and its deck to be clearly visible to a patron.

Reynolds tapped his fingers on his desk. "Down here, you not only have to prove negligence by the hotel, but you have to show that your client was zero percent negligent. We're still back in colonial times in Virginia. The hotel will do everything it can to show that your client should have done something to find out how deep the bottom of the pool was. If they prove that she also behaved even one iota negligently, they'll win. You'd better be sure you can prove that the hotel was entirely at fault. It's going to cost a bundle to sue Surfside International."

After the spinal shock subsided, tests showed that Skylar did not have a complete lesion of her spinal cord and would have some use of her arms and her right hand. She was transferred to the Kessler Institute in North Jersey. Her room there testified to how far the treatment of people with severe injuries had progressed.

Thirty-five years ago, Angelo Angarone had to rely on nursing aides and family turning him at least every two hours to prevent bedsores from developing. Skylar's specially designed air mattress had a timer that automatically inflated and deflated different parts of the bed. Near Skylar's bed was a Hoyer lift, a hydraulic machine with a sling that made transferring a patient from bed to a wheelchair much easier than using a monkey pole, which required strength that an incomplete quadriplegic like Skylar would not have. A power wheelchair with a joystick to adjust direction and speed, and buttons that allowed the user to change the angle at which the chair reclined and the height of the chair, sat in a corner of the room. Angelo's wheelchair had no adjustments and had to be propelled manually. There was nothing better in the seventies.

"I want you to tell me the truth," I said. "Your parents care for you a lot and want to do everything for you." Skylar nodded and looked me in the eye.

"Were you unaware that the section of the pool into which you prepared to dive was shallow?"

"That's true."

"Why did you decide to dive into the water rather than simply taking your time and wading in slowly?"

"Because I felt it would be the best way to adjust to the temperature difference in the water."

"Why did you dive in?"

"People at the other end of the pool were up to their waists and people in the middle of the pool were up to their chests. The number on the wall where I dove in looked like an '8.'"

A week later, I told Richard Reynolds what Skylar had told me and he filed a complaint alleging negligence against Surfside International Beach Hotel. Surfside responded, denying responsibility and blaming Skylar.

Dr. Matityahu Marcus, a professor of economics at Rutgers University, appraised the economic loss that Skylar would sustain because of her permanent disability. He estimated that her loss of income would be between 1 and 1.3 million dollars. A life care plan prepared by a rehabilitation and home care expert estimated that it would take 7 million dollars in present day dollars to pay for home care, medical care, evaluations and medications, equipment, supplies, transportation, and home modifications that Skylar would need during the rest of her life.

Five months later, Surfside International answered the interrogatories that were served with the complaint. Its pool was not scheduled to open until the weekend after the band trip, but the manager made extra efforts to fill it so the students could use it. The water level was high because it did not have time to recede. The pool deck had been repaired and the deck numbers had been scheduled to be repainted the following week. They said the information had been conveyed to the person from the parents' group who made the reservations. That scenario placed responsibility on the parents who arranged the accommodations. Surfside's allegations were designed to enlist the sympathy of jurors who might not feel inclined to punish someone who was doing somebody else a favor.

The day before Skylar was to be questioned orally under oath, John and I drove to Virginia to meet with Reynolds. "I think we have a chance to resolve the case," he said. "Surfside's lawyer pulled me aside at the City Club. He's read Skylar's interrogatories, Judy and Claire's witness statements, and the wage loss and life care plan. He's going to suggest to his client to attempt mediation. Everybody has too much to lose."

Not only had the medical profession made progress in dealing with seriously injured patients, but the legal profession also had made giant steps. Litigants now had access to information and statistics that permitted a calculation of damages likely to be awarded by a jury, using factors such as the amount of the medical bills, the extent of lost wages, life care plans, and the chances of success under local laws. Moreover, retired judges had joined organizations that offered mediation of disputes. Judges with experience handling complex cases like Skylar's assisted in settling a case so that both parties to the lawsuit would not be subject to the vagaries of a jury verdict. In Skylar's case, mediation would reduce the expense and inconvenience of presenting a case in Virginia, since most of the caregivers were from New Jersey.

The next day, we rode an elevator to the fifth floor and headed to the meeting room that would be used for the deposition. Skylar's wheelchair hummed softly as she used the joystick on one of the armrests to maneuver deftly through hallways. We entered a conference room with a large conference table. Skylar took her place at the table; Reynolds and I sat on either side of her. "Ready for your deposition?" Reynolds asked Skylar.

She nodded.

"Okay, then. Just remember what I told you. Restate the question in your answer so that it's perfectly clear what you are responding to, and don't volunteer any information that you are not specifically asked."

The defense attorney shook our hands. I remembered that whenever anyone had stood near Angelo in his wheelchair they towered over him, forcing him to look up at them and producing an uncomfortable psychological effect. Now, with Skylar's power wheelchair that could adjust its height, she stood nearly as tall as the defense lawyer. Her face was set in a mask of resolve and concentration. She was applying the same competitive drive that she had channeled to succeed at Holy Spirit.

The defense lawyer was wearing a striped dark blue suit, a white silk shirt, a solid red tie, and rimless glasses whose edges were so polished that they gleamed. He sat next to the court reporter on the opposite side of the table from us. Skylar testified about what had happened on the day of the accident and what her life was like now. When the three-hour deposition ended, Skylar was exasperated. She said, "I felt like I was the one on trial. He was attacking me, accusing me somehow."

Maureen spoke up. "Maybe we should be thinking about a settlement? We just want this to be over with. I'm worried about Virginia law and slick lawyers. Maybe settling with the hotel is the best solution. Is that possible?"

A settlement held a lot of advantages—it could be kept private with a confidentiality agreement, desirable because it would keep away the kind of "friends", the kind that came to look for a cut of the settlement money. A settlement would also allow Skylar to receive her award in a structured settlement as opposed to a lump sum paid out all at once. The money awarded a severely injured person like Skylar was intended to cover expenses for the rest of their life and if it was paid out in a lump sum, she risked blowing through it if she did not follow her life financial plan.

Finally, of course, there was the issue of going to trial, which is always a chancy proposition. The risk was even greater where the jury would tend to disbelieve the client or the law allowed the defense a powerful argument. Unlike the case of Linda, whom you will meet later, who had run the risk of the jury seeing her normal outward appearance as a sign that there was nothing wrong with her, Skylar had obvious disabilities and challenges to face. Would a jury decide that she had acted negligently in not determining how deep the pool was and cite Virginia's contributory negligence doctrine as a reason to give her nothing? A jury might sympathize with Skylar for her injuries and emotional suffering and award her hundreds of millions of dollars. Or they could compensate her for her economic loss, but nothing else. Or they could blame both Skylar and Surfside International and award nothing.

I asked Reynolds to find out if Surfside International was willing to mediate. They were.

It was a nonbinding mediation, so if no agreement was reached, the case would proceed to trial.

During the early stages of Skylar's case, Peter Antonuccio, a certified videographer, videotaped the staff at Kessler Rehabilitation Institute teaching Skylar to regain some of the independence she had lost. He filmed a physical therapy session that helped develop muscles to compensate somewhat for the parts of her body that didn't work anymore and drills for her arms—special boxing exercises and arms circles. In an occupational therapy session, Skylar struggled to pick things up, dress herself, and use a slide board, a special elongated piece of wood with a hole at either end. One end is positioned on a bed or sofa and the patient is then slid along the board on her backside to a wheelchair.

In an interview, Skylar's face revealed traces of the vibrant girl that she had been. But the bags under her eyes and the serious expression on her face bespoke how much had been taken out of her as she said, "I've tried to maintain a positive attitude—that's the most important thing. Sure I've gone through short periods of downward spirals. My boyfriend of three years broke up with me five months after my accident. I've lost touch with most of my other friends, too. Judy and Claire were supportive at first, but once they realized that I was not going to get better, they gravitated away. One of my friends stayed a little longer, but once she figured how hard it would be to take me even somewhere as simple as the movies, she stopped hanging out with me. She straight up told me, 'It's going to be a lot of work to hang out with you,' and nowadays I only talk to her once every two months or so."

Skylar paused and collected her thoughts. "When the doctors first told me about the extent of my injuries I never thought, 'This will be my life.' I thought that within a month I would be better. When I heard I was going to Kessler, I thought it was going to be like in Harry Potter, with all the patients in wheelchairs hurrying every which way. I'm not going to let my injuries deter me. I was used to training hard for the band. I'm gonna use my competitive drive to recover as much as I can."

I sent copies of the video to Surfside International's lawyer. To prepare the Quinns for the mediation, I hired Joseph DiGangi to help them gain an understanding of what kind of settlement figure they could expect. Joe was a structured settlement expert who designed settlements that were invested in stocks and mutual funds and paid the client annuities. By providing a settlement range, he could temper their expectations so they could understand whether an offer being made by the defense was reasonable or not.

"There have been a lot of cases where people have gotten large sums but lost it all very quickly," Joe began. "There are three major groups of people at high risk for losing large lump sums—lottery winners and those who cash out their retirement plans and lose all their money. They can go back to work. But you, Skylar, belong to the third at-risk group: people with catastrophic injuries. Your ability to support yourself with a job will be limited, so it is extremely important that any settlement is designed to last you your whole life."

Skylar nodded, understanding, but Kevin expressed his doubts. "Why shouldn't a bank or an investment firm like the one that handles my company pension get the money?"

"The money is invested in guaranteed, conservative annuities that grow with inflation," Joe explained. "They provide for needs like home caretakers and a weekly or monthly income to replace wages that Skylar will not be earning. Annuities insure a dignified lifestyle. I try to foresee any possible problems that could emerge, even years down the line, and then budget for them using the settlement money. The idea is to establish a yearly budget financed by a small portion of the return on the investments made using the settlement money. It's important to live within this budget and not rely on constantly withdrawing money from the principal. We call that 'feeding the bear.' The more you take out of the principal, the less it grows and it might not be able to grow fast enough to support all of your needs."

Joe paused and raised his hands in the air, gesticulating deliberately. "The money will be to make you whole."

"How can I know what a reasonable amount for me would be?" Skylar asked.

"That's what I'm here for. I will balance your needs and your wants. You might want the Taj Mahal, but my first concern will be to allocate money for a house that fits your needs. If you wanted something fancier, or if you wanted to pursue a particular interest, that can be budgeted for, but the important thing is to plan it out. Sticking to a plan is what's important. Withdrawing money as you see fit without regard for a budget is the best way to go broke."

Maureen shifted in her seat. "How much should Skylar be expecting?"

Joe showed them several colorful graphs and flowcharts representing the valuations that several experts had done. "Certain sums you won't be able to recover, like the 4.7 million dollars in medical bills your insurance has already paid out. In a 'you can't lose it case' like one in which a tractor-trailer hits a car in the rear, fifty million dollars has been the highest recorded verdict for a quadriplegic who had no use of his limbs and no sensory feeling. Verdicts range from ten to thirty million dollars, diminished by the percentage of negligence attributed to a victim," Joe explained.

After Joe left, I was confident that Skylar, Maureen and Kevin understood the range of possible verdicts and what kind of settlement offer would be acceptable and how the money would be invested and spent to ensure that Skylar's needs would be taken care of.

I described what a mediator did. Kevin was familiar with the procedure from labor negotiations and pointed out to Maureen and Skylar that when the mediator told them something they did not agree with to be calm and not to get angry.

On a Saturday morning, Richard Reynolds and I were on the fourteenth floor of the Virginia Trust Company building in Norfolk. Large glass windows framed a harbor filled with battleships, guns at the ready. Patrol boats with armed sailors circled the entrance to the harbor, a reaction to the World Trade Center tragedy of September 11, 2001.

We had come to the office of McClellan Consultants to present our case to three focus groups. I would present Skylar's case and Reynolds would argue Surfside's. The focus group would discuss the good and bad points in a room with one-way mirrors. The "jurors" had received an invitation to participate and were paid fifty dollars for the day. They were the type of people that made up the jury pool that would hear Skylar's case.

At the end of the day, we had learned that most of the jurors loved Skylar. They believed that Skylar did nothing wrong. Reynolds had argued that the "SWIM AT YOUR OWN RISK" sign exonerated Surfside and that the parents who knew that the pool was not completely ready should be responsible. Jurors who favored Skylar were parents, those in helping professions, and minorities. Those who sided with Surfside were single men and women, business owners and military personnel. The mock jurors were asked to make a monetary award, assuming Surfside was 100% at fault. The awards ranged from ten to twenty-five million dollars.

Skylar, Maureen and Kevin were encouraged to decide what to accept before we went to mediation because the pressure at the mediation tended to negatively influence decisions. We agreed that if Surfside's insurance company made an offer of fifteen million dollars, it would be acceptable. Most likely, a claims committee at Surfside's insurance company was following a similar procedure.

Judge Nathan Shusted had bushy eyebrows, deep-socketed eyes and a pleasant voice. "Good morning," he said to the Quinns, Reynolds, and me.

"I do not like to have the parties meet each other until there is a settlement.

Oftentimes, people say things that they regret later. Everything you tell me is confidential and nothing that is said by any party can be used for or against you in court. Do you have any questions?"

"Not really," Skylar said.

"I'll go now and talk to the Surfside folks and will be back."

Judge Shusted shuttled back and forth during the morning, sharing Surfside's view of the case, admonishing us that "Virginia law isn't good for plaintiffs," "Norfolk is a military town and very conservative." "Folks here don't make a lot of money like you do up north," "You didn't sue the parents' group."

Fortunately, our preparation before the mediation caged emotions that would have otherwise upset Skylar, Maureen and Kevin.

After lunch, Judge Shusted invited Reynolds and me to meet with Surfside's representatives. He slid across the table a prepared agreement that provided for a settlement of $17,000,000. Seven million dollars would be used to purchase tax-free annuities to fund the life care plan and compensate for loss of wages. Lump sums paid now would cover attorney's fees and the cost of building an addition to the Quinn's home better suited to Skylar's needs. Lump sums would be paid every five years for as long as Skylar lived.

Three years after the settlement, Skylar says that the money allows her to do what she wants, go on trips and buy things for myself. "Of all the patients with spinal cord injuries I met in hospitals, the ones with a positive attitude were the most successful. I met one patient at Kessler with a bad attitude, 'It's over for me,' he said. 'There's no hope.' But he was the exception and not the rule."

"I can drive." She motioned in the direction of the minivan with handicapped license plates in the driveway. "I just got my license and am looking forward to being able to drive again. My car has a driver's seat that slides out so I can just drive my wheelchair in and get behind the wheel, and it's steered by hand controls."

Skylar smiled. "I've been taking classes at a local college for two terms. I want to train to be a reading specialist."

"School takes up a lot more time and it is harder for me to keep up. However, the professors give me extra time to take tests. Before the start of a semester, I send out emails to the students in my classes and explain my situation. I tell them that I have trouble writing down notes and that I need someone to take notes for me. I always get at least four or five responses. People on the whole are very helpful. I've learned to ignore those who stare because they don't understand my injury, but there are far more who will smile and pick something up for me if it falls or open a door—people are very understanding."

Skylar's experiences with rehabilitation were very different from the way things used to be. Now, through the efforts of people like Christopher Reeve and organizations such as the Miami Project to Cure Paralysis founded by the Buoniconti family after Marc, the football star, was paralyzed, increased awareness of spinal cord injuries had led to better fundraising and more research. The medical field had made giant steps since the days when Angelo was confined to a wheelchair. Skylar lives with the knowledge that her life isn't over because of her accident.

"How did you feel about the legal process?" I asked.

"On the whole, happy," Skylar answered. "Pleased that I was able to get a settlement. To this day I haven't even told my older sister about it, because she likes to gossip and would probably spread the word that the hotel had given me so much money."

As she talked, I reflected on how the legal profession had changed from the time when I was starting out. Back then, few lawyers were highly specialized in a particular field, such as catastrophic injury. There were no directories to point someone looking for representation towards an attorney who had experience with their specific problem. The transition from "cowboys to specialists" that has taken place over the past thirty years has given people access lawyers who actually understand their injuries. Back when the Angelo Angarones and Bobbie McKenzies of the world were looking for someone to fight for them, they had to rely on not much more than word of mouth. Since then, the legal system has come very far in ensuring that every person is properly represented.

Skylar backed away from the dining room table at which we were sitting and turned towards a hallway with closed doors. "Let me show you my new room," she said.

Her bed had aquatic-themed covers on it, and her Hoyer lift stood to one side. On her desk was a computer that she spends a lot of time on. She rolled a strange looking mouse with the tracking ball positioned on top rather than on the bottom. "I use this special mouse because I can't grip a normal one. When I'm on the computer I like to surf the Internet and play fantasy baseball. I also like to play baseball on the Nintendo Wii." She motioned to a dresser across from her bed which had a TV attached to a thin white video game console.

"Because the Wii uses a special remote that can detect motion rather than a traditional handheld controller, I can strap it to my arm and play baseball on it." She smiled. "It's a way for me to temporarily forget about my physical limitations."

Computers are a powerful tool for the seriously injured. They helped Skylar. She had made friends through her involvement in the online world.

"I almost forgot to tell you!" Skylar turned on Skype and dialed. "Good morning, Sky," Skylar said. "Good morning, Sky," a man in a wheelchair with a headrest, breathing through a ventilator attached to his throat, replied. "My lawyer's here. Show him your cockpit." The camera scanned a room that looked like an airplane cockpit. "I'll see you in a while, Sky." Skylar said. The screen went blank.

"He's a C-3." A C-3 quadriplegic has lesion more severe than Skylar's. "He can't move his arms and needs a ventilator to breathe, so he lives in a special cocoon. He controls his environment by means of a tube into which he blows air. He even works collecting money for a local college by phone, inside his cocoon. He calls me Sky Queen. I have lots of friends on the computer." When I grew up in the 1950's, Sky King was the aircraft pilot who was the star of an adventure series. He captured criminals using his plane called Songbird.

At the door, Skylar said, "My life isn't as bad as people think it is."

Several weeks later, summoned by Skylar's excited voice, I knocked on her front door. After a momentary pause, the door inched open. A large golden retriever gripped the inside doorknob. Skylar wheeled into view. "Do you like Prince? I just got him. He's a service dog from Canine Companions for Excellence, a California company. He knows more than forty different commands, like turning on lights, picking up dropped keys and opening doors. I just got back from a special two-week course to learn how to interact with him. We have a very special bond already. I love him."

Skylar Quinn had come a long way since the day that she plunged headfirst into that pool of shallow water. In the 1950's, Skylar would not have done any of the things that she is pursuing or have the hopes and aspirations that she holds for the future. She would not have had all of the equipment that made her life easier and more independent. She benefited from the lessons learned by those who suffered before her.

3. ONE IN A MILLION

"Open wide," Mary said, feeding a spoonful to Amber, her two year-old granddaughter, the apple of her eye. Mary had spent the afternoon making pasta fagioli for her traditional Friday night family dinner. She cooked celery, onion, garlic and parsley over medium heat in a large saucepan, then stirred in chicken broth and homemade tomato sauce and simmered it. She added pasta, cooked it until it was tender, added undrained beans, and sprinkled grated Parmesan on top. She served her daughters, Felicia and Paula, and Sal, Felicia's husband, Amber's father.

After dinner, Felicia and Paula helped store the leftovers. Sal was still washing the dishes.

"It's past Amber's bedtime. You go home with Paula," Sal instructed.

Felicia carried Amber to Paula's small Japanese Datsun and put her in the back seat. From the front stoop, Mary waved goodbye.

While Mary's family was sitting down to dinner, Karl Lamont, having finished a hard day's work on the construction crew for a nuclear power plant in Salem, New Jersey, had stopped at the Jack of Diamonds Tavern on Route 40, a two-lane cement highway connecting Salem and Pennsville, to join his co-workers for a "thank God it's Friday" drink. He shuffled to his car, parked in front of a giant cement mushroom, started it up and pulled out of the parking lot onto Route 40.

Three miles later, as he rounded a curve, clockwise in direction, he saw a car cross over into his lane. The sound of the crushing metal was deafening.

At Mary's house, Sal finished the dishes and set out for home. When he saw a line of cars backed up, he thought, "Another roadblock." Route 40 was a "drug way" for smugglers avoiding the aggressive state police who made "profile stops" to confiscate drugs being transported from the south to north Jersey and New York. He turned onto a side road to avoid being delayed and when he pulled into his driveway and saw no lights on, thought that Paula must be caught in the line of cars backed up by the roadblock.

Only minutes later, a Pennsville police car, its wigwags spinning and siren screaming, sped down Route 40. Karl sat in his car, injured, but not seriously. "The other car," he told the policeman, pointing to a small Japanese model with smoke rising from the debris. "It came into my lane, right in front of me."

Ambulances and rescue personnel were summoned; Paula, Felicia, and Amber were extricated from the wreckage. Amber, who had taken the brunt of the impact, was rushed to the Alfred I. Dupont Institute in nearby Wilmington, Delaware for treatment of her life-threatening injuries. A CAT scan showed massive bleeding in the skull and a rupture of a membrane at the base of the skull. The two year old, her black eyes fixed in a sea of white, was attached to a respirator and placed in an incubator. Paula, Felicia and Karl were taken to a local hospital for emergency treatment. Paula had two fractured ribs and a gash on her forehead that took twenty stitches to close. Felicia had bruises on her arms and a stiff neck. Karl had a separated left shoulder that was placed in a sling.

Sal drove back to the scene of the roadblock, where a tow truck was chain lifting a crushed Datsun. A Pennsville policeman had examined the bald rear tire on Paula's car and concluded that Paula had spun out and traveled into Karl's lane. Sal nervously approached a kneeling policeman, chalking the area in Karl's lane where debris had carved out a point of impact. After he identified himself, the policeman told him that his daughter had been gravely injured and was clinging to life. "Where is she?"

"Dupont."

Sal ran to his car, its engine still running.

Another Pennsville policeman caught up to him. "Turn off the engine. I'll take you. You're in no shape to drive."

The kneeling policeman completed chalking, then photographed the scene and returned to police headquarters, where he completed a rough draft of an incident report and put it in the IN box of his supervisor. He took no statements from Paula or Felicia. It was simple. Paula was at fault. He mailed a careless driving ticket to Paula. In his mind, the case was closed.

While Felicia, released from the hospital the next morning, spent day and night with her daughter, envelopes with medical bills piled up on the dining room table. New Jersey's No-Fault Automobile Insurance Law provided for payment of medical bills for any person involved in a motor vehicle collision, but neither Felicia nor Sal was in a state of mind to fill out forms.

A social service worker at the hospital told Felicia that because the bills weren't being paid, arrangements were being made to transfer her daughter to Ancora Psychiatric Hospital. Felicia stiffened, alarmed. Felicia had visited Ancora during her nursing training and remembered it as depressing, dirty and filled with the rancid odor of an unventilated medical ward. She had witnessed the poor care given at Ancora. Felicia would never send their daughter to a warehouse for people "sick in the head." As tears filled her eyes, the social service woman said, "Felicia, I suggest you contact a lawyer."

"A lawyer? What lawyer?"

In the 1970's, there were no directories or Internet sites that listed lawyers with experience in counseling brain-injured people, not even the now ubiquitous billboards and television advertisements. Now, organizations that helped brain, spinal cord and burn victims popped up. The social worker at the hospital did some research. I had represented members of the brain injury support group and had spoken to the group. The social worker recommended that Felicia call me.

In the Dupont Hospital Pediatric Trauma Ward where I met Sal and Felicia, Amber lay motionless. Her round face, with eyes widely spaced and a nose pert like on a doll, didn't have a blemish. Her hair was combed flat with a part in the middle. A doctor explained that she was in a coma and that on the Glasgow Coma Scale, which rates the severity of a person's injuries, he had rated her a "3", the lowest score. The Glasgow score helps determine whether a person will live or die.

Felicia, a nurse, collapsed into a chair at Amber's bedside. The doctor knelt down and, holding her hand, asked if she wanted to hear more. She nodded. Amber's CAT scan showed that her tentorium, a part of the dura membrane which covers the cerebellum and supports the occipital lobes, had ruptured and filled her brain with blood. Amber had suffered one of the most catastrophic kinds of brain injuries. Her chances of survival were one in a million.

I told Sal and Felicia that they would have to deal with Paula's insurance company if they wanted to seek compensation. Sal's black eyes, deep set beside a prominent nose, wandered. "I don't want Paula's insurance premium to go up. She's suffered enough." Tears welled up in Sal's eyes. "It was my fault that I let Felicia go home with Paula."

Felicia's lips tightened. Her beautiful, olive-skinned face was drawn. Adamantly, she said, "What happened was not Paula's fault."

"Not her fault?"

"No." Felicia said that as Paula approached the curve, lights of another car drifted into their lane. "I yelled 'Watch out' and Paula turned to her left to avoid the oncoming car. I think the other driver saw our lights and pulled back into its lane."

On my way home, I stopped at the Pennsville police station to pick up the accident report. What if the other driver was at fault? There would be other insurance available. The officer who had been at the scene told me the report was not completed. He repeated what Karl had told him, adding that the vehicles were in a junkyard around the corner from the police station, impounded because of the possibility that the accident would end up a fatality.

"If the baby dies, the careless driving ticket issued to Paula is going to be changed to vehicular homicide, a criminal offense. She should spend some time in jail. Putting a kid in a car with a bald tire is a like playing Russian roulette," he said, his jaw jutting out.

At the junkyard, I took pictures of the vehicles. My photographs would show a very bald rear tire on Paula's car.

The glove box in Karl's car was open. Reaching in through a window, I leafed through some papers that revealed that the car was leased by Karl's employer and was insured for one million dollars. If I could I prove that what Felicia said was true, I might be able to make a difference in the lives of Amber and her family.

A veteran New Jersey State Trooper I knew suggested I take a course in accident reconstruction at Northwestern University in Evanston, Illinois taught by J. Stannard Baker, author of the leading book on the subject. I combined a visit with my high school tennis doubles partner who lived in Chicago with a three-day course at Northwestern. I sat in a room with about twenty lawyers. Speakers talked in gobbledygook about something called SMAC, a simulated model of automobile collisions sponsored by the National Highway Safety Council with mathematic formulas that measured things like coefficients of friction that made roads slippery, tire construction that caused a car to hydroplane in water, and yaw characteristics of cars and trucks. My mind wandered. Maybe Albert Einstein would understand the speaker? On my left a Detroit attorney bit his fist. To my right, a squat, partly bald man squinted through metal rimmed spectacles. Nothing I heard the first day had anything to do with the crash that injured Amber. I told the registrar at the end of the day that I had had enough and asked for a refund. As I turned to leave, an intelligent looking man approached me. "Why are you cutting out?"

That's when I learned that the first speaker in the morning, Albert Fonda, would be presenting a topic that would interest me.

Fonda, a man in his fifties with an oval face, had a thin mustache arched over a strong mouth. His nose was pushed in like a fighter. He talked about CRASH, which stood for Computerized Reconstruction of Accident Speeds on the Highway. It was a new process he had developed to reconstruct how an accident happened. Using measurements of car damage and computations of the weight of the cars involved in a crash and the weights of the passengers in the cars, he claimed he was able to calculate speed, angles of impact and the momentum of spin.

Karl's and Paula's vehicles were still impounded, scheduled to be sent to salvage a few weeks later. Fonda, an engineer who specialized in dynamics, agreed to visit the junkyard with me, take photographs, and measure the "crush" to determine the speed and angle of impact.

A few weeks later, I entered Fonda's office which was in a non-descript strip shopping center. As he escorted me through a narrow hallway he said he believed Felicia was telling the truth. In a room at the end of the hallway was a machine that looked like a piano. Fonda turned a switch and fed cards with holes in them. Paper flowed like a Teletype. Fonda spread the sheet of paper on a desk. "Both cars were traveling about forty miles an hour, ten miles an hour below the speed limit. The angle of impact shows that the driver of the Datsun yanked the steering wheel to the left and that the driver of the Oldsmobile was pulling to the right. When a car travels around a curve that bends to the right or clockwise, it has a tendency to drift left, counterclockwise." Fonda fingered a small model car and placed it on a diagram of a curve and showed me how Paula's car would behave if she yanked to the left and what Karl's car would do as it rounded a curve. Sure enough the cars collided just where the pictures of the damage showed. Okay. If I had a hard time understanding Fonda, would a jury think that CRASH was hocus-pocus?

Sal and Felicia's reaction to this new information was not what I expected. "We only want our daughter back. We don't have a chance in court. We live here and know how the system works. No one is going to believe an expert who you pay to testify. Policemen in Pennsville are gods down here. We're not going to fight a Pennsville cop. They're good people."

When a medical insurance payment was late, Felicia called me. A telephone call to their automobile insurance company solved the problem because New Jersey's No Fault Automobile Insurance Law provided that medical bills for anyone injured in an auto accident were to be paid regardless of fault. But her calls became more complex. She wanted to keep Amber at home, where she could take care of her, but the reality was that it was impossible to care for a person in Amber's condition without special training. Amber could not be left alone. She had to be turned every two hours to prevent bedsores. She wasn't expected to live more than a few years due to a circulatory problem, which caused her hands to turn blue. She had to be fed and bathed like a baby. She needed to be aspirated regularly to prevent lung complications.

Felicia had to work; otherwise, she would lose her job. She and Sal relied on her salary. Felicia looked everywhere for a place that could care for Amber, and was politely told that the situation was hopeless and only Ancora Psychiatric Hospital was willing to take Amber in. Felicia considered sending her to the Institute for the Achievement of Human Potential in Philadelphia, which had a controversial program for brain-injured children, but which had been roundly criticized by the medical establishment. The Institute claimed it could teach paralyzed brain-injured children to crawl, creep, even walk, that it had made blind children see and read, and teach children who could not speak to talk.

Feeling Sal and Felicia's frustration, I contacted a neuro-pediatrician on the medical staff of the Children's Hospital at the University of Pennsylvania who had cared for my son. He told me that Amber's injuries were so pervasive that the Institute would not be able to help Amber and that it would be a waste of money and lead to even more frustration. He suggested the Lynch Home in Willow Grove, Pennsylvania, a facility founded by a woman whose child needed excellent long-term care. It was an extremely difficult decision. Felicia and Sal felt as though they were abandoning Amber. When the Lynch Home, a private non-profit organization, asked for assurance that its charges would be paid, Felicia told them to call me.

I set up a conference call with insurance representatives and the Lynch Home and made sure that the Lynch Home had all the information it needed to process its bills and that, though located in Pennsylvania, it was understood that New Jersey laws would provide lifetime coverage for Amber. But I had not been paid a cent. I had paid for a course in accident reconstruction and the services of an expert, and I had not acted purely out of the goodness of my heart. I wanted to succeed.

So when Sal wanted to see me, I thought that perhaps he was bringing me a present to show their appreciation. But Sal walked into my office empty-handed. "I've had second thoughts," he said. "The more I think about what you told us— about Felicia telling the truth—the more I want to sue the bastard."

A few days later, Sal and Felicia signed a contingent fee agreement. If I collected any money on behalf of Amber or Felicia, I would get twenty-five percent. If I did not recover anything, they would not have to pay me anything. I filed a lawsuit alleging that both Paula and Karl were careless and the cause of Amber and Felicia's injuries. Even though I would argue that Karl was the cause of the accident, I had to name Paula because the police officer's report would become part of the case.

My telephone rang. An angry Mary was on the other end. "How dare you sue my daughter? You are going to break up my family. That's all I have left."

Minutes later, Felicia called, panicked that her mother thought she was ruining her family. I explained that Paula, who had suffered mild injuries, had the right to counter sue Karl. I gave her a list of three personal injury lawyers in whom I had confidence and, shortly thereafter, Mary contacted one of the lawyers and hired him.

Defense lawyers retained by insurance companies representing Karl and Paula filed a response to my lawsuit. The law provides that parties can ask each other questions to discover facts about a case. To their written questions, answered under oath, Paula replied that she had no recollection of the accident. Karl's response repeated the police report: "Paula's vehicle came into my lane of travel and collided with my vehicle."

Karl also stated that he was hospitalized and released. I obtained the hospital records. To my surprise, a routine blood test showed that Karl had consumed more than two beers, enough alcohol to put him over the legal limit. I could show that a drunk caused the accident.

At the depositions, Karl sat across from me in a conference room in his lawyer's office. A clean-cut man in his mid-twenties with the arms of a weightlifter, Karl looked like someone who would be believed by a jury. He said that he finished work, went to a tavern, had a beer, and was on his way to the motel where he was staying when Paula's car came into his lane. Then he volunteered. "I got out of my car and went over to her car. I stood at her window and asked her if she was all right. She told me she was okay, that she was sorry—that the accident was her fault."

"Will you repeat that?" I asked. "Do you understand you are testifying under oath, that you swore you would tell the truth?"

Karl repeated what he had said. His neck reddened. He leaned forward. "You are damned right I am telling the truth. I have nothing to hide."

But he had locked himself into a bold-faced lie. Hospital records and reports of personnel at the scene of the accident showed that Paula was unconscious at the scene of the accident.

I didn't confront Karl with the evidence of alcohol. I would wait until trial and spring it on him then. I would show the jury that he was not only a liar but also a drunk.

After deposing Karl, I met with the doctors who had treated Amber, all specialists and professors. I had to learn more about how the brain functioned and how Amber's brain injuries had affected her. I listened to Amber's doctors at Dupont explain that every part of Amber's brain had sustained serious damage.

Finally, I spent two days with leaders in the personal injury field discussing the art of motivating a jury to render a large verdict. Million-dollar verdicts were still a rarity. Bill Colson, a Miami lawyer known as Million Dollar Bill, advised me to send my evidence to Karl's lawyer, who would relay it to the insurance company he represented. "I'm sure you'll get a sizeable offer," Colson said.

Karl's lawyer responded with an offer of fifty thousand dollars. "Nuisance value," he sneered. "I'm making the offer not because my client is responsible. That's how much it will cost to defend the case." He paused. "If I were you, I'd take it. Your client won't live to see her day in court. Besides, to get an award, you have to prove your client has conscious pain. The poor kid is a vegetable." But Betsy Braun, who cared for Amber at the Lynch Home, assured me that Amber did have "some level of feeling," even though it might not be conscious and that she would be able to demonstrate it in court.

During the two years it took for the case to come to trial, Amber contracted a series of illnesses that almost took her life. Pneumonia. A staph infection. Stomach ulcers. Meanwhile, doctors at Dupont Institute who would be needed to testify told me, one after another, "We don't go to court. We are too busy treating patients and teaching."

New Jersey had not yet adopted a rule permitting expert witnesses to be videotaped. New York and Pennsylvania had recently adopted such a rule. I requested the Court to permit me to go to the doctor's offices with the defense lawyers and record their testimony on film. Judge George Farrell, a first-rate lawyer before being appointed to the Bench, ruled that filmed testimony would be permitted in the courtroom.

The filmed depositions of the Dupont doctors were so dramatic that even the defense lawyers were speechless. Three doctors displayed the CAT scans and with a model of the brain explained how the blunt trauma that Amber suffered caused bleeding which put so much pressure on the skull that it killed brain cells in almost every area of the brain. They all agreed that she would need twenty-four hour care and that it would be a miracle if she survived more than a few years. They testified that Amber responded to touch, but that her response was only a reflex action like swallowing and breathing. "Does she feel anything?" I asked each doctor. "Not consciously," they replied. The defense lawyer didn't ask the doctors a single question or try to discredit them.

Walking out of the Dupont Institute, Karl's lawyer, a tall, imposing man, said, "Even if you win, I'll appeal Judge Farrell's ruling. Don't forget what I told you. Fifty grand will look awfully good a few years from now." His deep voice was enough to shake a glass sitting on a table.

I played my trump card. "I'm going to prove your client was drunk," I said. "No you aren't." Karl's lawyer chuckled, then added, "Paula came into his lane. Drinking didn't cause the accident."

As the trial date approached, Karl's lawyer made motion after motion, requiring me to file answering briefs and to travel back and forth from Trenton to Salem, where the court that had jurisdiction over the case was located. A three-hour trip, I had to leave home at six-thirty in the morning so that I would not be late for Judge Farrell, who called his court to order promptly at 9:30 a.m. When I tried to contact the nurse who had drawn Karl's blood, I learned that she had died. Now I knew why Karl's lawyer had said, "No you won't" after I had played my trump card. I was faced with an imperfect chain of control of the evidence. Because I would not be able to prove that the container in which the blood was drawn was properly refrigerated before it was analyzed, the jury would never hear about Karl's drinking.

On a sunny April morning, my suitcases were in the trunk of my car and the legal briefcases filled with documents and exhibits sat on the back seat. I put on my red and blue "court tie" and tied the laces on my worn brown cordovans—the pair I always wore to court, even with a blue suit, because they brought me good luck. I checked into the motel where I expected to stay for two weeks.

Judge Farrell asked, "Have any offers been made to settle this case?"

"Fifty thousand, Your Honor."

"What is your demand?"

"A million dollars, Your Honor. That is the policy limit," I said.

"I guess we're going to have a trial," Farrell said, rolling his eyes.

I was sitting at the plaintiff's counsel table when Sal tapped me on the shoulder and asked to speak to me outside. In the hallway, he said, "We can't bring Amber to court. She's come down with pneumonia."

I closed my eyes and took a deep breath. "Let's keep that to ourselves."

Defense counsel for Karl and Paula made their way to their counsel table. Judge Farrell waved to them and pointed to his chambers door.

"What's happening?" Felicia whispered.

"The judge is going to try to get the case settled."

"I hope so. We'll accept whatever they offer. We just want this to be over. Money isn't going to change anything. Amber is what she is. She is never going to get any better." Sal nodded.

The defense lawyers came out of the judge's chambers wearing poker faces. Judge Farrell asked me to approach the bench. Leaning forward and in a voice just loud enough for my clients to hear, he said, "There's no offer. The fifty thousand is withdrawn. You still have the fifteen thousand from Paula's insurance company if you want it."

I had spent almost twenty-five thousand dollars and hundreds of hours preparing the case. Had Karl's lawyer heard about Amber's illness?

The clock had struck 11 a.m. when the panel of jurors entered the courtroom.

My heart was pounding when I stood up to give my opening statement. I looked each juror in the eye. Four years of work and worry was about to pour out.

"Ladies and gentlemen of the jury, Felicia will tell you that Karl lost control of his car." Holding a model car in my left hand, I made a clockwise arc like Albert Fonda had done, saying, "The centrifugal force on the car as it rounded the curve on Route 40 pulled it into the lane in which Paula was driving, causing Paula to take evasive action. Karl will tell you Felicia is lying. It will be up to you to determine who is telling the truth. Karl has sworn under oath that Paula told him at the scene of the accident that it was her fault. Hospital records and testimony of people at the scene will show that Paula was unconscious from the moment of the collision until she reached the hospital." I explained the tragedy that had befallen Amber and Felicia. I took a deep breath and sat down, expecting Karl's lawyer to address the jury.

Instead, Judge Farrell called counsel into chambers and suggested to Karl's lawyer that now was the time to begin talking seriously. When I returned to the courtroom, I noticed a gentleman I had never seen before sitting in the back row. Karl's lawyer greeted him. The representative of the insurance company. Now was the time to talk.

The offer was if I would agreed to accept $150,000 if I lost and limit the insurance company's payment to $300,000 if I won, we could try the case only on the issue of responsibility, negating the need to present medical testimony or to bring Amber to court. "The insurance company knows that you can never predict what a jury will do. But it thinks its chances are much better than yours," Judge Farrell told me. No offer was made to Paula. The offer had its advantages. The case would be over in two days and the only witnesses would be Felicia, Paula, the police officer, Albert Fonda, and Karl. I would recoup the money I had expended and earn a small fee.

But any chance of a settlement evaporated when Mary told me, "I can't let my daughter let her sister go home empty-handed. How could she live with herself?" Felicia did not want her sister to feel that she was guilty because, in her heart, she did not believe she was. Negotiations went on, back and forth. Karl's lawyer informed me that the case could not settle and that I should be prepared to present testimony in the morning.

A Sheriff's Officer handed me a note. It said, "Call your father at the office."

My father, a "lawyer's lawyer," often gave me good advice and when I reached him, he told me that an appellate court had just ruled that an employee working away from home and who had housing supplied by his employer was considered to be in the course of employment if he was in an accident. If that were the law, Karl's employer would be responsible for any verdict over one million dollars if the jury found Karl at fault. He urged me to tell Karl's lawyer that I would claim that Karl was working for his employer at the time of the accident since the employer had rented the car and paid for his hotel room. Karl's employer was worth hundreds of millions of dollars.

Before we left the courtroom, I followed my father's advice. Driving away from the courthouse on my way to lunch, I saw the insurance company representative and Karl's lawyer walk into a restaurant together. Back at the counsel table after lunch, I heard footsteps behind me and then felt a hand on my shoulder. Karl's lawyer bent over and whispered, "The case is settled."

"Settled?"

He ushered me into the rotunda outside the courtroom, where he informed me his client would pay $950,000 of the million-dollar policy. Karl's employer did not want to risk being held responsible for Karl's carelessness.

$650,000 was awarded to Amber to be held in a trust. $200,000 was awarded to Sal and Felicia for the loss of their daughter. $100,000 was awarded to Paula for her injuries, which left her with an ugly scar on her forehead. Medical and institutional costs would be paid for the rest of Amber's life, calculated by medical experts to be five years at most.

A few months later, when I handed a substantial check to Sal and Felicia, she said she was, "Relieved. And excited. It's like we hit the lottery."

I winced. The lottery word was being used by insurance companies to demean lawyers and large verdicts in order to set the stage for reforms that would take away rights of people like Amber, Felicia and Sal. Still, in my mind, the case was closed.

A month hadn't passed when Mary called.

"They've found their dream house."

Mary worried that while Felicia and Sal had the money to buy the house, they did not have the funds to maintain it. Despite her warnings, they followed their whim. "You should have tied up their money like you did Amber's," she said, angrily.

Shouldn't the money sought to compensated the loss or damage to a life be used to make one whole, not to be able to purchase homes and cars? There was nothing in the law that said that. I had fought my heart out for Amber, Sal and Felicia. It dropped like a stone into my stomach.

Felicia and Sal resisted a plan for managing the money. Felicia bought expensive houses and cars, without considering the upkeep such things required, and her money ran out. Five years after the settlement, she and Sal divorced.

What was missing from Sal and Felicia's marriage? What caused money to drive a wedge between them? Did they substitute buying items for the missing piece? Was it the loss of a daugher. Or something else? Why had I not insisted on psychological or spiritual counseling?

Felicia remarried a year later and had another daughter, Natalie. Sal died of liver disease in Texas shortly thereafter. When Natalie was only two years old, Felicia was killed in an automobile accident.

"What do we do now?" Mary asked.

I had a court appoint her as Amber's guardian. In the years that followed, Mary called, sometimes frantically, when medical bills weren't paid, or when she thought the doctors were killing Amber. Although she was given only five years to live, Amber hung on. So did Mary.

Fifteen years had passed since Mary had become Amber's guardian, twenty years since the settlement. Mary's small, spotless colonial kitchen was filled with the fragrance of a fresh pot of coffee and apple crumb cake. On the table a newspaper headline screamed out about Terri Schiavo.

"Amber could have been sent down the same path as that Schiavo girl," Mary said. "Same injuries." "Her husband ought to be shot. Only God can take a life."

Mary had not always sung that song. When Amber's condition was ripping apart a marriage and a family, Mary had berated the doctors whose heroism had kept Amber alive.

"Thanks to the settlement, Amber had excellent care at the Lynch Home." She leaned forward on her elbows. "Isn't it a shame that Felicia and Sal went through their money so quickly?" Mary's eyes watered. "Who could have predicted that Sal would die before Amber, let alone Felicia?"

Mary had been waking up in the middle of the night thinking about how Amber's sole heir was her half-sister, Natalie, Felicia's daughter from her second marriage. Natalie had never shown any interest in Amber, never shown any independent motivation to visit her, and the few times that she did go with Mary, she did nothing but sit by a wall and mope.

If Amber died, Mary did not want "Amber's money" to meet the same fate as Felicia's and Sal's. She wanted to be able to limit how much Natalie could withdraw at a time.

"You know when you die without a will, the State dictates who gets what. Amber can't make a will. She's helpless. So what should I do?"

Even after withdrawals, there was over a million dollars in the trust. While Mary had been appointed Amber's guardian in the event of her parents' death, there was no provision for what would happen when Mary passed away. No one anticipated Amber surviving as long as she had. If Mary died, the State would become Amber's guardian.

Although the accident had taken place almost three decades earlier, and the case was settled twenty-five years ago, for Mary it wasn't over.

A week later, I pulled up to the subdued, middle-class neighborhood in Willow Grove, Pennsylvania and headed towards one of the few lawns on the block without any Halloween decorations. I was here to see Amber and to find out about a guardian to replace Mary.

The Lynch Home looked like a three-tiered wedding cake, each story shorter than the last and stacked neatly on top of one another. Abigail, a woman with a lined and seemingly careworn face, let me in. Her gray hair was neatly styled, and she wore a purple shirt and jacket made of a heavy fabric. The interior of the house was inviting, with soft pop music filling the enclosed front porch, which served as an entry hall. A few brightly colored pictures and Halloween decorations hung along the walls. In the next room was a bed with a blue striped mattress with a photograph of what looked to be a seaport above it. A protective blue pad covered a red brick fireplace. There was no smell—no smell to invoke images of a hospital ward, no smell to suggest this was anything but a true home.

There were nine patients at the Lynch Home, all severely retarded. Amber was the only one whose injury was the result of trauma; the others were victims of drugs or birth defects. Amber had had the same roommate for her entire stay at the Home. Amber's functioning hadn't changed much in twenty-eight years, but she had grown and matured. The small staff treated Amber, like the other residents, as family, but Amber was actually lucky because her real relatives visited her two to three times a year, more frequently than other families. Though it was not yet Halloween, her aunt Paula was already inquiring about when the Christmas party would be.

I was led through a corridor, past a refrigerator with pictures of some of the Home's other residents, to a room with blinking lights hung on the wall and Christmas carols playing through another speaker—perhaps it was meant to be therapeutic? Amber's wheelchair was in the middle of the room. She was strapped into a wheelchair because her brain injury had destroyed her ability to balance. She had black, close-cropped hair and wore a black, sleeveless blouse with an orange spider on it, a green shirt underneath, a denim skirt, knee-high socks, and red and white New Balance shoes. My first thought was how small she looked. She was thirty, but looked barely half her age. Her feet were little, almost dainty, and she appeared to be no more than five feet tall.

Betsy Braun, her caretaker, walked up close and started speaking in warm, reassuring tones as she introduced me.

"Is that a smile?" she asked.

The corners of Amber's mouth turned up slightly and then her tongue stuck out. While Betsy talked to her, Amber rolled her head. Front and back. Side to side. I sat on a couch, watching. She had Felicia's olive skin and dark eyes and Sal's profile. Amber rolled her head towards me, and for a moment one eye stared at me. Betsy continued speaking and leaned in close. Amber rolled her head once more and stared straight at her.

Betsy had explained that Amber had usable vision, adding sarcastically, "Whatever that means."

"Did she see me?" She certainly seemed to react. She didn't like a lot of contact, especially on her arms, which Betsy illustrated by taking hold of Amber's right arm, which made Amber somewhat agitated as she pulled her arm back. She lifted her left arm, ran it through her hair, and put her fingers in her mouth. Betsy gave her a kiss on the cheek.

She sat still in her wheelchair as Betsy explained that she attended a special school until she was 21, where she developed her muscles and joints through sensory stimulation to allow some normal movement. She could sit up in her wheelchair without any help. Betsy gestured to devices lining one side of the room designed to allow Amber to stand for short periods of time. She had a job, or at least that is what the Lynch Home staff liked to call it. State law required that the patients be out of the Home for at least five hours every day, so she was taken to different places. The key word was normal. The Lynch Home staff tried to enable Amber and the rest of the residents to have normal experiences. They took them to parks in the summer, on rides into the country and to puppet shows.

I didn't know what to say. A yellow book sat on a table. I picked up The Little Engine That Could and began to read. When I looked up after "I wish I could, I wish I could," Amber's eyes were closed and her head tilted.

I bid Amber a silent farewell. I went back through the corridor, past the pictures on the refrigerator, back into the entrance hall, down the steps, and past the bare lawn. The next step was to get a Court to accept the recommendation, supported by Mary, that her daughter be appointed guardian—so that if Amber continued to live beyond Mary's years there would be someone to look out for her welfare. I could not come up with a solution to Mary's concern that the half-sister might blow "Amber's money."

A few months later, her aunt was her guardian.

I was sentenced to wait for the next frantic call.

4. IF ONLY

"No drinking and driving."

"No problem, Mrs. Rich."

"Terry's father wants to take you. And pick you up."

"Mom. We're grown-ups," Terry exclaims in a huff.

"Okay. Have a good time. Be careful. I'll be waiting up for you."

Terry throws his arm over his friend's shoulder. Philip, short and stocky, wearing a white leather jacket with Panthers Football embroidered on its back, limps to a 1980 Oldsmobile parked at the curb, the broken left leg that sidelined him from his linebacker position just out of a cast. That afternoon, the Panthers defeated their archrival, the Tornadoes. Now, they are on their way to a celebration party at Jackie Bell's, the team's co-captain.

Terry, clad in a denim jacket and black jeans, slips into the front seat and waves to his mother. "Parents can be a pain," he mutters.

Philip fingers his car keys. "Your mom's a piece of work. You're the most independent guy I know and she's on your case?"

"It's not my mom. It's my dad. He was all over her at dinner. You just got your license last month. He wanted to take us to the party. He didn't want me in your car at night. My mom stood up for me. My dad was in a huff. It wasn't pretty."

Terry's mother, Nina, shuts the front door, waving. Philip keys the ignition and flips the radio switch. "Time after time." Cyndi Lauper's voice is mellow. "We can do better than that." Terry pushes a button. "That's better," he adds, hearing Madonna sing, "Like a virgin," in a rock and pop style. Philip pulls away from the curb.

On her way to the kitchen to finish washing the few dishes that are left, Nina taps Frank, slumped in a chair, on the arm. "Terry's gone, Frank. "I know," Frank, his eyes affixed to the television screen, responds in a tone filled with disgust. A superintendent at the Band-Aid factory, Frank does not like not getting his way.

Nina joins Frank, watching Different Strokes. NBC's Saturday night lineup—Gimme A Break, Partners in Crime and Hot Pursuit will occupy them until Terry comes home, at which time he will join them, laughing at Saturday Night Live, and then tell them about the fun he had at Jackie Bell's.

Three miles later, Philip turns right onto South Road, a two-lane macadam road. Terry spots a bend in the road ahead and glances at the speedometer, which reads 25 mile an hour. "You're being a good boy," he says. Philip glances at Terry. "For your mom," he teases, and then focuses on the road. The right wheel of the Oldsmobile lurches. A flat tire? Philip muscles the steering wheel to the left. The Oldsmobile yaws and heads across the road. Philip slams the brake. The car rolls over, and over and over again. Terry's head takes the brunt of the impact with the telephone pole.

Police cars, their wigwags spinning, speed past farms and cookie-cutter housing developments that are attracting city folk escaping from the servile etudes of New York. Volunteers respond to a radio call and head to the firehouse. Rescue vehicles and an ambulance fire up. The strains of U2's In the Name of Love break the quiet of a moonless night.

A policeman shines a flashlight into the Oldsmobile, dust and debris settling like smoke from a just extinguished fire. He tries to open a door. It doesn't open. Backup arrives and light up flares. Yellow-suits place Jaws of Life on the passenger door and push, pull and yank, freeing an opening for a paramedic to get close to Terry, who doesn't move. "What's your name?" he asks and gets no response. He observes shallow breathing, blood seeping from ears and shines a pen light into fixed eyes.

Immobilizers are around his neck. Boarded, he is carried to a gurney, which is rolled into the back of an ambulance and attached to the floor. A paramedic places a mask over Terry's nose and mouth and turns a knob on a tank labeled Oxygen. A siren wails as the ambulance rolls away.

In the front seat of a police car, Philip hands his license to a policeman and answers questions. "I felt my right rear drop down. Like a blow out." "I was going about 25." The policeman takes notes and tells Philip to stay put. Then he ambles over to the wreck and flashlights the speedometer, stuck at 40.

Frank's eyes close while he watches Gimme A Break. Nina nudges him. "Go on up. I'll wait up for Terry." Frank grudgingly trudges upstairs.

At the Medical Center, doctors follow a gurney out of the Emergency Room. Now, Terry has tubes attached to his stomach and his arms. In an operating room, doctors activate a respirator. X-ray machines roll over.

Nina is startled by the ringing telephone. Who is calling at this time of night? Maybe Terry isn't having a good time? He's not on the football team. Maybe Philip did have a few beers? "Hello?"

"Son of a bitch," Frank barks as he pulls his pants on. "Son of a bitch. I knew. I knew."

By the time Frank and Nina reach the Medical Center, an intra-cranial pressure bolt has been inserted into Terry's head. MRI's find a brain stem injury. Internal bleeding is under control. Multiple facial fractures are yet to be managed. Terry's left eye is nearly hanging out of its socket. He is comatose.

Nina's reaction is so violent that the hospital staff thinks that she is having a heart attack and admits her to the Cardiac Care Unit. Now, Frank has two people on his hands.

In a tiny fluorescent-lit room, a doctor informs him that Terry's condition is grave, that it can change any minute and that it is important for him to call the family to the Center. Outside the room, in a hallway, is a telephone booth. Frank punches the wall before he enters and dials.

Three days later, Nina is released from Cardiac Care. While "if onlys" circle inside her head, she fumbles newspapers and magazines on a table in the Intensive Care waiting room. She comes across an article in The Trentonian about a lawsuit I had filed on behalf of a brain-injured child.

Pursuing cases where a change in product promoted safety not only ignited my interest, but also had provided me with funds to expand my staff so that I could provide the service that so many families I met while Ellen and Jared were being treated in New York needed. Florance Churchill, a legal assistant at a law firm that specializes in family law, answered an advertisement I had placed, seeking a social worker to counsel people with serious injuries. Burned out from working with families on cases that she described as ones "where nobody is a winner," Florance displayed the qualities—intelligence, the ability to listen, and caring—that one needed to work with people in crisis, whose lives had been changed in a milli-second.

Florance and I were reviewing a report that Richard Wolf and Howard Gage had prepared in a case in which a forklift operator lost his hand when it was cut off in a "guillotine like" reaction when he pushed a load that had gotten stuck. My office door was closed. Nancy knocked and then opened my office door to peek inside. "Can you be disturbed? A woman is calling from the hospital. Her son was in a bad accident."

Nina Rich's voice was shaky as she related what happened to "my Terry."

A short woman with a wide face and a serious expression walked through the solid double doors that opened from the Intensive Care Unit. A man with a head of white hair shuffled behind her. My outstretched hand greeted them. "Albert Stark."

"Nina Rich." Turning, she said, "My husband, Frank."

"I'm so sorry to hear about your son."

"Thanks for coming."

I followed them into a room over which was a sign—Family Room. Nina and Frank sat on chairs lined up against a wall covered with blue Leatherette. I pulled a chair a comfortable distance away from them. Frank gazed into space, scratching his neck with hands that appeared very large. Beneath Frank's forehead were hooded eyes.

"What happened?"

"Frank was upstairs. He had just gone to bed. I was watching television. The phone rang. It was the call every parent dreads." Her voice trailed off. Frank choked on his words, "If only I had driven Terry and Philip myself. By the time we reached the hospital."

Nina continued, telling me what had happened since they arrived at the Medical Center and what Philip had told them about how he lost control of his car, thinking he had a blowout, braking and pulling the steering wheel hard. Frank's right hand fisted and he stomped his foot. "Do what you can do for us."

I knew what he meant. Get us money. But how?

Northwestern University sits on the Lake Michigan waterfront, about thirty miles north of Chicago. While handling a case, which required a reconstruction of a two-vehicle collision, I sat in a classroom for a week, listening to J. Stannard Baker, who had authored a well-known text on the dynamics of auto accidents. Engineers who specialized in many aspects of accident reconstruction, such as calculating speed from the damage to the vehicles, and the lack of coefficient of friction that made roads slippery even when dry, spoke.

John Serth, a road engineer from Albany, New York, described what happens when a car drops off a road surface and the driver wrestles with the steering wheel to gain control. Serth, lecturing about federal and state regulations that provided that a road drop-off was unsafe if it exceeded two and a half inches, had described exactly what happened to Philip.

The next day I arranged to meet Serth at the scene of the crash. It was still fresh with ruts and debris. Examining the drop-off where Philip's Oldsmobile went off the road, Serth exclaimed, "This is a killer road," and then explained that a curve in a road should have a shoulder or a feathered edge since when a car rounded a curve, especially a narrow one, it was not unusual for a rear tire to go off the paved road. The road had recently been repaved and its edge had not been feathered, as required by the New Jersey Department of Transportation. Serth opened a large suitcase containing cameras, measuring devices, and a Plaster of Paris kit. Serth photographed, measured, and made a mold of the drop-off where Philip's wheel fell into a ditch that shouldn't have been there.

Township records revealed that the road had recently been repaved. I started to think that I had a case against the Township for improper repair of the road. I contacted Frank and Nina, and agreed to take the case.

At first, the evidence didn't mean much to them. Their only concern was for their Terry. He was still comatose. His life hung by a thread. Nina maintained a vigil, seeing to it that Terry was turned every few hours so that he would not develop bedsores, which if infected, she was told could lead to his death.

Seldom did a motorist, especially a newly licensed driver like Philip, have enough insurance to pay for what Terry would need. After I successfully handled Amber's case, about a dozen families, whom I could not help either because they had no case or because there was not sufficient insurance to make pursuing a case worthwhile either for the family or me, had contacted me.

After I learned more about Terry's injuries, that they would be permanent and that he would never be able to live independently, I questioned whether paramedics, doctors, and nurses should take such "heroic measures" to keep someone in Terry's condition alive. Ethically, the Hippocratic Oath requires it. I sensed that the road ahead for Frank and Nina would be difficult and frustrating, with the chances of any meaningful recovery for Terry little to none. I also perceived that Frank and Nina would want to keep Terry alive at almost any cost. Not only did they love Terry, but also they were also wracked with guilt. "If only," they repeated time and time again to me.

While Terry lay helpless at the Medical Center, Frank became increasingly angry. Not at Philip, but at the Township government. Frank wrote a letter to local newspapers to complain about the road condition. Other residents joined his crusade for safer roads. In response, a township councilman referred to Frank and those who wrote letters supporting his concerns as miscreants, and compared their cause to that of people who insisted on maintaining homes at expensive New Jersey seashore resorts and then expected state and federal assistance after hurricanes damaged their properties. Frank became angrier and more intent on "getting" the Township.

During the six weeks Terry was at the Medical Center, he did not wake up.

Spending time with Frank and Nina, I got to know Terry. The summer before the accident, he had toured the country with his choir. He visited the Metropolitan Museum of Art in New York to see exhibits about the Vikings and King Tut. He had taken apart computers and electronics, motors and transmissions, to see how they were made. He had operated a ham radio since age thirteen. At fifteen, he learned to install burglar alarms and started a burglar alarm installation company complete with letterheads and business cards. At seventeen, he took his brother's Corvette, which had lain in pieces in the garage, and put it back together. At eighteen, Terry had his whole life ahead of him.

Terry's sister, with a bouffant hair-do and blue mascara and deep red lipstick, confided, "I was 17 when Terry was born, so I'm a bit older. I watched him grow up. Terry is more like a son than a brother."

Terry's brother eyed me. "Me and Terry were best friends. Everything that went on in our lives, each of us knew about. We told things to each other that we told to nobody else except each other." With a high forehead, strong neck, and muscular arms bulging a grey sweatshirt, he picked up pictures. "This is me and Terry. You can even see just by the pictures we are alike because we dressed alike, our hair was alike, and we both had mustaches. I got the idea of a mustache from him because he always had one and I always looked up to him for everything, so I guess I grew one, too, to be in his image."

While representing Angelo, I had encountered my share of ethical and moral challenges. I questioned whether I was suing Allstate Seat Cover Shop just to get Angelo money. When I discovered that had Allstate spent four more dollars and an hour and a half more to recondition the seat to the manufacturer's specifications, Angelo would not have been in a wheelchair, I felt not only justified, but also intent on making the business own up to its responsibility.

I talked candidly with Frank. What would happen if a jury found Philip and not the Township responsible for the accident? Wouldn't jurors think that a large verdict would affect them as taxpayers?

"The township violated the law. It too should pay, just as you might pay a fine for a traffic ticket. If I park ten minutes too long and my meter runs out, I get a ticket. I pay the fine." Frank was insistent. Frank urged me to file suit, focusing on the Township government's responsibility and downplaying Philip's role.

The case was uncertain in my mind. I didn't question the ethics of Frank's strategy to sue the Township. Cases take at least two years to reach trial. Rehabilitation would end in less than a year and a half. Rehabilitation would be an oasis in a desert. Terry would grow to manhood, but his passions and dreams and goals would never be realized. For Frank and Nina, watching him grow older, never having a life, would be difficult. I understood Frank's concerns. He was at his wit's end. Not knowing how he was going to cope with a disabled son, I didn't question the ethics of this strategy.

The Medical Center personnel determined that Terry could not be cared for at home, that there was nothing more it could do. Terry was transferred from acute care at the Medical Center to a rehabilitation center an hour away from Frank and Nina's home. Terry was still comatose when he was transferred and remained comatose for seven months. Every day Nina made the long drive to be with Terry.

Frank became more and more distant, silent and edgy. He buried himself in his work at the Band-Aid plant. Nina suggested he seek help, thinking that his anger toward her was because he blamed her for not letting him take Terry and Philip to the celebration. "I'm going to lose my husband and son," she told me one day, tears streaking her cheek. Frank didn't want to hear about going to a doctor. "There's nothing wrong with me," he said.

During an extensive rehabilitation program, Terry recovered some ability to speak. But his brain injuries manifested themselves in severe ways. His memory suffered to the extent that often he could not remember people who had visited him just hours earlier. He often could not keep track of what time of day it was. Initiation and motivation skills were also impaired. He would not begin performing specific, necessary behaviors by himself—basic things like getting out of bed in the morning, brushing his teeth and getting dressed—but instead he had to be cued to begin performing an action and then had to be constantly encouraged to continue following all of the steps to carry out the action.

He also experienced persistent, explosive episodes of violent behavior directed at himself and others. The outbursts included hitting his head, pulling his hair, and occasionally striking at or trying to bite others. They averaged ninety times per week with sometimes 280 in a single week. They were devastating.

The involuntary, violent behavior was especially resistant to change. The doctors caring for Terry tried various treatments to curb these impulses, but with no noticeable results. "Dyscontrol" was the medical term used to describe the condition. It meant that Terry was not even fully aware of the damage he was doing to his own body when the violent episodes occurred. All this meant that Terry could not live self-sufficiently, despite moments when he could speak or think clearly. It also meant that Frank and Nina could not care for Terry at home.

New Jersey's automobile insurance law helped people like Terry. Every New Jersey driver paid approximately twenty cents a week for a benefit that paid medical bills for seriously injured people for the rest of their lives. Terry was eligible for the best care available. Florance shopped long term care facilities with Nina. A facility that could handle Terry in upstate New York, while three and a half hours away, fit the bill.

Florance and I asked each other, "Now that we have Terry taken care of physically, what's the use pursuing the case against the Township?"

"If Terry was killed, Frank and Nina would have rights to compensation," I said.

"Terry is someone who can be described as 'living dead,'" Florance quipped. "He is a different person from the one who got into the Oldsmobile."

"You're right," I said. "And, if we win the case, it will wake up other towns to the importance of getting rid of killer roads."

"Okay, how are we going to win the case?"

I had a flashback and leaned back in my chair. "Did I ever tell you that one of my summer jobs during college was with a street paver?"

"You're kidding me," Florance said. "You? Paving streets?"

"Yup. I ran a roller behind a Barber Green, the machine that lays the asphalt. It was the worst job I ever had. It was hotter than hell." I chuckled. "That's probably why I decided to go to law school."

"You know how roads are paved?"

"City streets, yes. A rural road, no. Maybe we should find out. Call the Township police department and see whether there are any construction road closures. We used to have a cop car behind us on all our paving jobs to warn oncoming cars that we were working."

A few minutes later, Florance stuck her head in my door and said, "We're on our way."

In the distance on a rural township road, a red police car bubble flashed. A policeman signaled me to switch lanes to go by a paving crew. In front of the paving crew was another police car with flashing lights. "I guess we can't watch what they do," Florance said, disappointed. I shrugged my shoulders and then noted a farm stand entrance and turned in. "Where are we going?" Florance asked. "Follow me," I said.

Slithering through rows of corn on a hot July afternoon, we reached the area where the paving was being done. I separated corn stalks so that we had a clear view of the paving crew. Florance whispered, "Peekaboo, I see you!" She reached into her over-the-shoulder handbag and pulled out a camera. It was July 7.

A portly man with a red hard hat unrolled sheets of paper and signaled to the driver of the Barber Green. A roller followed. The red hat and two men wearing yellow hard hats and carrying rakes walked behind the roller and began to feather the asphalt the way John Serth had described.

Florance grabbed my elbow. "They know how to do it the right way," she said. She pointed her camera and snapped.

At Health North, only certain staff members, whom Terry knew and who had looked after him for a long time, could work with him. Terry's family worried. What would happen when his favorites retired? How would he adapt if his family decided to transfer him to a facility that was closer to home?

Nina learned of a brain-injury support group at the St. Lawrence Rehabilitation Center in Lawrenceville, New Jersey. She became a regular attendee. She listened to a forty year old wife talk about her husband's loss of memory, his inability to pay attention to her, follow instructions or plan and organize his life. A mother complained about her son, who cursed at her and smashed dishes and who, just minutes later, didn't remember what he had done.

In 1980, the Brain Injury Association of America was founded. Nina joined the New Jersey chapter. She discovered that other families were in the same boat, being tossed about navigating rough seas. She became more and more aware of the unique challenges of living with a brain-injured person. The symptoms never went away. The patient seldom got better. Nina and Frank would always be at the mercy of Terry's caregivers. It was fine so long as the people taking care of him did their best to do a good job, but what happened if budget cuts or personnel change ravaged a facility? A brain injured person that could not look after himself, like Terry, never had the option of leaving like a healthy person would. He obviously could not look out for his own interests and keep the staff from ignoring its responsibilities. Winning in court became important to Nina as well as Frank.

As the trial approached, no offers were made. I made an overture to the Township attorney to settle, hoping for a quick resolution to the case so as to help Terry's family get started with the process of moving forward with their lives as quickly as possible. No offer was forthcoming. Oftentimes in cases of severe injury cases, the injured person and his family want to get the legal process out of the way as soon as they can. The difficulties of coping with grief and adjusting to a new and very different way of life are enough without the added complexities and distractions of a trial. In this case, however, it seemed like that would not be a possibility. Frank was adamant.

I prepared to go to trial. Philip testified in a deposition that he turned the wheel sharply because he felt one of his rear wheels drop off the road and he needed to compensate. His testimony fit hand-in-glove with Serth's findings that the "killer road" was unsafe. Still, would this evidence be powerful enough to convince a jury? Would they buy the Township's attempt to turn Philip into the scapegoat for what happened?

Four months later, the day of trial arrived. I could see the grave concern in Frank and Nina's eyes. Their facial expressions reflected all of the difficulties they had gone through without wavering. They had already put Terry's needs above their own. While I had no doubt they would always stand by Terry, a verdict would make their life easier financially.

Judge Samuel Silver invited the Township attorney, Philip's attorney and me into his chambers. "Any chance of settling?" he asked.

Philip's attorney offered one hundred thousand dollars, the limit of his insurance.

"No pay," the Township attorney said. It is all Philip's fault. He just got his license and didn't have enough night driving experience."

Five days later, I approached a jury of three men and three women. "The importance of this case to Terry Rich and his family is inescapable," I said. "Terry will not be able to speak to you or appear in this courtroom because the Township didn't follow its own rules. The Township casts blame for its carelessness on Philip.

"Terry had his whole life ahead of him. Frank and Nina Rich have lost the son that they loved and who loved them. They have lost his ability to guide them, counsel them, and care for them as they age.

"Terry is not the person he was on the afternoon the Panthers beat the Tornadoes. The old Terry died. I stand here today as an advocate for someone I can describe to you as a person who is 'living dead.' At the end of the case, I am going to ask you for a verdict in Terry's favor against the Township in accordance with the laws of New Jersey. I am asking you to send a message to governments everywhere to get rid of killer roads so that other Terrys won't have go to hospitals, rehabilitation centers and long term care facilities."

Nina, wearing a sky-blue cotton blouse with an open collar, sat in the witness stand and looked at the jury through large plastic rimmed glasses. "He was a special kind of kid. He was trustworthy. With his hands, my Terry could do anything. Computers, electronics, motors," she said.

Frank raised his right hand, placed his left hand on the Bible, and swore to tell the truth. He held back tears and rubbed his ears. "I've got all these memories of him and of course I can't talk about him, the way he was and the way he is now, only because I can't control my emotions." Sad eyes told his story better than his words.

A video screen rolled in front of the jury box. A doctor with gray hair and a full beard fixed his eyes on the camera. Terry sat beside him in a wheelchair. "He's very, I think, very sensitive to the presence of his family and has benefited greatly from their visits here at the rehabilitation center, and receives a lot of emotional support from them. They play a primary role in his rehabilitation here. And the sad reality, however, is that I don't think he is fully aware of their absence when they leave; that his memory is such that he doesn't really comprehend the fact that they were here, and that they've gone, the fact that they are no longer here."

An expressionless jury exited the courtroom as the first day of trial ended. The next morning, John Serth explained why federal and state regulations required feathering of asphalt on rural roads and showed the photographs and mold to the jury.

The Township's road supervisor explained that the road had not been feathered because he didn't think it would matter if a driver drove within the speed limit and was careful, then added, "And I did not know of the state or federal regulations. Nobody gave them to me."

It was time for cross-examination, the crucible of the truth.

"On July 7, just six months ago, were you supervising a road crew on South Lane?"

"Yes."

"Is South Lane a rural two-lane road?"

"Yes."

"Just like the road on which Terry Rich was injured?"

"Yes."

"Did the crew you supervised rake and feather the asphalt that was laid on South Lane?"

"Objection, your Honor," the Township lawyer barked, rising to his feet.

"The basis for your objection, counsel?" Judge Silver asked.

"Not relevant."

"The witness may answer. Objection overruled."

Jurors stirred, waiting for the answer.

I backpedaled to my counsel table and fingered Florance's photographs.

"Can you repeat the question?" the road supervisor asked.

"Did the road crew you supervised on July 7 rake and feather the asphalt on South Road?"

"Yes."

"Why?"

The road supervisor's Adams apple rolled in his throat. "Because after I was given the lawsuit I read the regulations."

In summations, Philip's lawyer argued that Terry's fate could not be blamed on Philip. He adopted my argument, telling the jury, "Ignorance of the law is no excuse." The Township lawyer continued to blame Philip, and adopted another strategy. "Ladies and gentlemen," he pled, "The Township has 75 miles of road. To feather the roads would cost our taxpayers a lot of money."

After I reviewed the testimony, my last words were, "This is a case where the Township broke its own rules. If you park at a parking meter too long, you get a ticket and pay the fine because you broke a rule. Now the Township must pay. The lawsuit has already led to safer roads. Hurting the Township in the pocketbook will make roads not just in the Township safer, but you will send a message to governments, federal, state and local. A verdict for Terry will prevent what happened to Frank and Nina's Terry from happening to someone else's son."

Two days later, an exhausted jury entered the courtroom.

"Ladies and gentlemen of the jury, have you reached a verdict?" the judge intoned.

"We have, your Honor," replied the foreman.

Frank and Nina closed their eyes and lowered their heads. Terry's brothers and sister clasped each other's hands.

The next day, the morning newspaper headline screamed, *Brain-Damaged Accident Victim Will Get $4.7M.*

That afternoon, Frank and Nina came to my office. "Surely the Township will appeal, but their chances of winning are slim," I said. I told them how Angelo, emboldened by his newfound financial freedom, feeling that he had hit the lottery, had spent beyond his means and was on his way to losing the money that he had been awarded.

At the urging of the American Trial Lawyer's Association and insurance companies, in 1982 Congress, with bipartisan support, had added a provision to the federal tax code that created an alternative to a large cash settlement called a structured settlement. It was a wonderful way to guarantee financial independence to a client like Terry.

The structured settlement enabled injured people and their parents to work with a lawyer and an outside financial advisor to determine future medical and living needs. In a structured settlement, an annuity is purchased from an independent third party that makes payments to the individual who has been injured. Unlike interest earned from a bank, structured settlement payments were completely tax-free. The annuity provided an after-tax rate of return that few investors could match.

"Locking up the money in a fund is the safest way to make sure Terry's needs are taken care of. You never know if the insurance company that is paying the long term care bills will go bankrupt or out of business," I said. "The money will grow over time, ensuring that Terry will be taken care of for many years. I think it would be a good idea to make you the legal guardians so that you, not Terry, will be able to withdraw funds."

Frank and Nina's eyes lit up. They relished the opportunity to care for their son in any way they could, be it by making sure he was being properly looked after at Health North or by managing his money. "I think it's a good idea. We'll do it," Frank said.

"This is the safest way to handle Terry's money. I only wish that more brain-injured people and their families who received large financial awards took this kind of care with their money," I said.

The appeal process dragged on for a year. Frank and Nina resented the fact that their friends believed that they were set for life and didn't have to worry about anything. Nina said to me shortly after the case was over, "Terry's money is not our money. While it hurt me to see the headline, I realize now that articles about cases educate people. If I hadn't seen the story of your case in the paper, I would not have called you, and who knows what would have happened if you hadn't gotten that man to come in from New York and analyze the road." She quickly added, "To the people who believe that the money makes our life easier, I have a question, 'How would you like to spend the rest of your life going to a nursing home...and Terry has to live like that?'" No amount of money could repair or undo the tremendous damage suffered by Terry and his family. I had no doubt that Nina and Frank would give all of it up to have their son back with them.

After the verdict was upheld, Frank and Nina were appointed guardians. They purchased secured annuities that would grow free of federal and state taxes, and keep up with expected inflation. Substantial sums would be paid to Frank and Nina, Terry's guardians, for his benefit every five years as long as he lived to insure against unexpected inflation. Terry would receive a monthly check to pay for things that would enhance his quality of life.

The case over, the "if onlys" were just beginning.

Weekends for the Richs had changed. Two hours after leaving their Cape Cod home, they drove past Scranton, on a winding road with mountains on the right and a lake on the left. They talked often about how close the family was before Terry's accident, how Terry's situation pushed the family members away from each other, how after having spent so much time in hospitals and treatment centers, they could not spend time together without terrible memories coming back, and how when they did get together, for holidays and family occasions, a pall of gloom, though unspoken, was always cast on the event. "When you have an accident like this, the whole family is in the accident, not just the injured person," Frank complained.

No matter the weather, to Frank and Nina dark clouds obscured the sky by the time they reached Health North, where an ambulance stood ominously by the front entrance of a brick building. On a typical visit, a patient usually sat silently just inside, past the electronic sliding doors that led into the building, a blank look on his wrinkled face.

The building itself had a sterile, lifeless quality to it. A few patients wandered aimlessly around the reception area. Their heads were bent low, their eyes staring at their shoes.

The Richs approached where a bored-looking woman sat leafing through some files. The woman looked up from her work and recognized the Richs instantly. They took an elevator up to Terry's floor. Gruff looking aides milled around, but none of them looked like they were in the mood to talk. Screaming, loud and disturbing, emanated from behind one of the other closed doors down the hallway. Several of the light bulbs in the corridor were burned out and consequently the lighting was dim and sinister shadows played along the walls. The floors are grimy and there are puddles of liquid in several places. The paint on the walls is chipped and peeling, and a window is smashed and being held together by duct tape. Budget cutbacks and disinterested staff have made Health North not the place it was when Terry first went there.

Terry's door is open. Terry sits in the middle of the room, watching TV. Nina's face contorts and she fights back tears. Terry is incontinent and had accidentally wet himself sometime before their arrival. Nina searches for a staff member to find out why Terry had not yet been changed.

A nurse follows her into Terry's room. "This is what I am talking about!" she exclaims, indignant. "We have to fight to get even a basic level of care for Terry. I thought that the fighting would end with the trial, but now that the quality of care here at Health North has gone down so much I just don't know what we are going to do."

An aide is summoned. Nina's alertness and persistence produced positive results. How much could the Riches accomplish when they had to fight the staff to get them to do their jobs? Even if they succeeded in making an improvement in Terry's care, surely they could not do anything for all the other patients, many of whom had been all but abandoned by their own families. These were the kinds of dark thoughts that crossed Nina's and Frank's minds as they left Health North behind.

At her brain injury support group meetings, Nina discovered that the Riches were not the only families that were disappointed with the level of care their loved one was receiving. The letters she had written to Health North fell on deaf ears. She got results when she visited but they were short-lived. The Brain Injury Association of New York took up her cause and put pressure on Health North to raise its standard of care.

A few years later, things had changed for the better at Health North. Another health care system acquired the facility. Nina was now satisfied with the level of Terry's care. She felt that there were good aides that worked with him, and that it was the best, not to mention, the closest place for him. Nina invited me to join them on a visit.

In front of a well-kept but modest Cape Cod house, I prepared myself mentally for the three and a half hour trip to see Terry. Frank answered the doorbell. In the foyer, he mused about how, when Terry first went to Health North, it was a model rehabilitation facility and how it had run into trouble, from bankruptcy to fraud and abuse charges.

"Institutionalized care is a frightening proposition," he said. Health North had come under scrutiny from accusations of inappropriate practices. "Funding at brain-injury facilities has been cut to a fraction of what it used to be; turnover is high and staff people come and go, making it difficult to establish continuity with regards to consistent treatment," he said.

Understaffing, poor training, and negligence were not uncommon. At these facilities, businessmen were the ones making decisions, not doctors, putting profits ahead of quality of service.

As I listened I thought that the solution to the problems that plague brain-injury victims was for everyone to do what Terry's family was doing—not to forget their injured relatives, and show them that they love and care for them. At the same time, the visitors were monitoring the care given at the facility. Nina must have been reading my mind because she stole the words right out of my mouth. "If everyone visited the people they've forgotten about, then there would be better quality of care."

On a cool November day, 2004, we headed towards my car. Nina approached and tossed a laundry bag into the back seat of my SUV. She had aged. She needed a step stool to climb in. "It's always good to see you. You never forget us." I had sent everyone in the family a birthday card for all these years.

"What's in the bag?" I asked.

"Clothes. Terry always needs new clothes to replace ones that he accidentally dirties." This motherly responsibility manifested itself in other ways as well as she told me, "I like to buy clothes as presents for my other children and I would feel bad if I left Terry out." She chuckled, "Terry has more clothes than anybody else at Health North."

We drove along the same scenic but lengthy route the Riches had been taking many times a year, for twenty years. Nina remarked wistfully that she wished she could see Terry more, but the truth was that there simply wasn't anywhere in New Jersey that could care for him. Health North was the closest facility that was equipped to take care of Terry—and willing to take him. As we talked and reminisced, I wondered, what is Terry like today? Will he know who I am? Will he recognize his family members? Will he even let me into his room?

The building's exterior looked cheerful and well kept. Inside, the lobby resembled a hotel. The room was softly carpeted and pallidly lit by wall lamps; quiet music played from hidden speakers. When we got past the lobby and entered the facility proper, the carpeting gave way to a clean white tiled floor.

While waiting for the elevator, I couldn't help but observe a staff that was efficient and purposeful. I could see some patients sitting in a colorfully decorated room, listening to music coming from a stereo system. Others were walking around the hall in which we were standing, getting some exercise. A strange, stale odor permeated the hallway, but at least it was not the stereotypical hospital smell of chemicals or unclean waste. "This place is cleaner and smells better than most others out there," Nina commented. The elevator arrived and we headed up to see Terry.

We paused by the half-closed door to his room and walked in. The room was comfortably warm. It was small and dimly lit, with the shades drawn. Most of the light came from what squeezed through the doorway and the television situated along the right wall on which an old sitcom was playing. A small white cot served as a bed. Above it was a bulletin board with a few pictures, including one of a much younger Terry with a manicured mustache, alert eyes and a broad smile, and another of Terry's niece at the prom with her date. In the middle of the room, sitting in a wheelchair at a small table with a tray of food on it, was Terry. He had unkempt graying hair and a bushy mustache and wore a black polo shirt with white stripes, purple sweat pants, and black sneakers. His left hand, curved inwards, hung limply at his side.

Terry looked up and saw me. A confused, scared look came into his eyes and he immediately started to grab his hair with his hand. Nina moved quickly to comfort him. Frank took his arm and said "Hang on to me, Terry." Terry complied, wrapping his right arm around his father's waist and averting the spasm. He said, quietly, "I'm sorry." Nina introduced me, explaining to Terry that I was his lawyer and that I was here to meet him.

"NO!"

The shout was so quick, unexpected and piercing – almost desperate – that I jumped in spite of myself. "That's OK, Terry," Nina responded soothingly. I had been warned that Terry was not receptive to strangers of any kind. Even though I had learned that this was because strangers took him out of the comfort zone of the world he had created for himself, I was still startled.

His nurse entered the room, having heard the shout.

After Terry calmed down, he simply ignored me. Nina encouraged him to eat his food, but he said that he wanted to go outside — something Nina said he always loved to do. Frank obliged and wheeled him towards the elevator.

The nurse answered my question, "How does Terry spend his days?"

"Terry can't walk. His brain injury robbed him of his ability to balance himself. He spends his days opening and shutting the shades in his room, watching TV, and playing with the TV buttons. Most of the time he is oblivious to the outside world. Terry's curse, however, is that he remembers everything of his life up to the time of the accident. He knows his family, where he used to live, what he used to like. When strangers approach him he is reminded of all that he has lost."

The nurse asked, "You want to hear more?"

"He likes to watch older shows like Sesame Street and The Price is Right, even shouting out bids on the various prizes. Generally when working with Terry, the newer staff needs to be accompanied by one of the older workers, who had worked with Terry since the beginning and who he trusts."

The nurse said that families often presented the most difficult challenges when dealing with brain-injury cases. Those patients who had been at Health North the longest were typically visited least by their families. The longer a patient stayed at such a facility, the more willing his family was to simply abandon him. This was unfortunate, because all of the patients liked to hear their families' voices, even over the telephone. Clearly, Terry's family was an exception to this general rule. They were tireless in their efforts to visit Terry. All of the nurses and aides agreed that this had improved his quality of life immensely.

I noted that Terry's room was brightly ornamented with Thanksgiving decorations, posters, pictures, and, of course, his beloved television. A glance down the hallway revealed that none of the other rooms had much decoration at all.

Terry and Frank returned from their trip. Terry had something to say, "This place sucks dick," he said, almost gleefully. "And what do you want to do?" asked Nina. "Fuck you." She didn't mind the cursing. "As long as he smiles and watches that TV he can curse all he wants," explained Nina. "I just want him to be happy."

Terry took a few more bites of his food and then asked to be taken out again.

I joined Terry and Frank as they walked around a few of the streets near Health North, circling around to get back to the facility. Terry read street signs and even advertisements that we passed. Each time a car drove by on the road, Terry would say what make and model it was. This was the most talkative Terry had been since we arrived. He seemed more animated and excited, livelier somehow, when he was outside.

We returned to Terry's floor and headed back towards his room. We got back to Terry's room and he ate a few more bites of his lunch.

Michael and Lisa, two people that worked with Terry, entered the room for a visit. Michael was actually on his day off, and Lisa left her job after giving birth. But both had come in just to see how Terry was doing. Michael had a reddish mustache and graying hair and wore a plaid shirt, blue jeans, and work boots. He was well built and had large hands. He was the only aide strong enough to support Terry when he got out of his chair and walked around the hallway, his only form of physical exercise. Michael thought of Terry as a friend or a family member, and treated him accordingly. The way he saw things was simple: treat him in the same way you would want to be treated if you were in the same condition.

"We're his friends," they said, emphasizing that last word. "We have to fill the void." As a result Michael and Lisa tried to care for Terry and made him feel good. Terry could pick up on others' emotions and react accordingly, so the people who worked with him made an effort to act cheerfully while around him. As a result, a bond had grown between Terry and Michael. They teased each other and even exchanged barbs. Michael realized how difficult it was for Terry, especially when he remembered what it was like to be at home, so he tried to make Terry feel as though he had actual friends at Health North, rather than just people whose job it was to take care of him.

Michael also believed in giving straightforward answers, regardless of whether those answers were good or bad. When Terry said, "I want to go home," Michael told him the truth, that is, that home was very far away, and that, even though his family would love to be able to bring him back and care for him themselves, Nina and the others were not able to do this. "Terry appreciates this straightforwardness," he said, "And understands the impossibility of going home."

Terry turned to Nina and said, "I love you mommy," then to Frank. "I love you, Daddy." He finished his food and drink and Frank and Nina and the aides prepared him for a nap. They helped him lie down and changed his wet underwear. Frank and I said our goodbyes.

As Terry fell asleep, Nina was the last person in the room. The rest of us stood outside, waiting for her to bid farewell to her son. Nina turned off the television, put on her coat, turned to face Terry's sleeping figure, and said, "Goodbye, Terry." Then she walked out of the room, and closed the door behind her.

Nina reached into the rural mailbox at the edge of her driveway. She thumbed the mail. "I have a pitcher of iced tea and some fresh fruit in the refrigerator."

While she poured tea and filled bowls with cut up pineapple, oranges, and apples, she said, "I get mail every week from the Brain Injury Association." She fingered a brochure, which she handed to me. Stem Cell Research. "It has been stifled in this country, mostly thanks to the lobbying of fundamentalist religious groups. A born-again Christian once tried to tell me that Terry's accident was God's will. I don't buy that. If they had a family member in Terry's condition, they would think differently. That's what I would tell those people who oppose stem cell research. Religion is a private matter and they should keep their convictions to themselves and not try to force them on others. Look at this one," she said.

I read, "Currently there are at least ninety thousand Americans with brain injury so severe that it requires an extended stay in a post-acute brain injury rehab, but there are only a few thousand specialty beds, and upwards of 90 percent of them are already occupied."

I looked up. She had a book in her hand. "Read what Superman has said." She slid Christopher Reeve's book to me. A passage was underlined. "It is our responsibility to do everything possible to protect the quality of life of the present and future generations. A critical factor will be what we do with human embryonic stem cells...They have been called 'the body's self-repair kit.' No obstacle should stand in the way of responsible investigation of their possibilities. In fertility clinics, women are given a choice of what to do with unused fertilized embryos: they can be discarded, donated to research, or frozen for future use... But why has the use of discarded embryos suddenly become such an issue? Is it more ethical for a woman to donate unused embryos that will never become human beings, or to let them be tossed away as so much garbage when they could help save thousands of lives? While we prolong the stem cell debate, millions continue to suffer."

When I finished reading, Nina said, "My Terry is a poster child for people like him. He's gone through both the ups and downs of institutionalized care." Nina took Superman's book from me. "Listen to this," she insisted. "If your young child or grandchild suddenly became paralyzed because of a spinal cord injury or brain damaged in an accident, would you be able to look him in the eye and say that research on the best hope of recovery is, in the words of Senator Brownback, "illegal, immoral, and unnecessary?" Senator Brownback of Kansas leads a coalition that opposes stem cell research.

I nodded my head up and down as Nina railed about the conservative politicians. "Superman tells it as it is, doesn't he?" she asked.

"There are not enough Health Norths," Nina said, explaining that Terry is lucky that at least now he is in a good place with a competent and dedicated staff, but not every brain injured person is that fortunate. If the government spent the money its spending fighting wars on the disabled, the unfortunate, I don't care if they are diabetics or kids in the cities with mothers and fathers on drugs..." Her voice trailed off. Nina's eyes danced. "If only," she said.

"If only...." Frank said.

As much as Terry's life was a tale of a few seconds that changed everything, I saw it as a tale of strength and perseverance by his family, who never abandoned him, and never ceased to look after him and care for him. Terry's family, deeply affected by what had happened to him, dedicated themselves to caring for him and helping in his life as much as they could. Now I saw it as a plea to help others before it was too late. If only…

5. A ZIG-ZAG LIFE

Anthony Rosati—Rosa's father—was a union plumber. "Carbon monoxide poisoning from the gas heater," he said, in my office, killed his daughter. "The gas company that supplied fuel for the heater. If they had inspected the heater, they would have seen a yellow flame and known something was wrong." He slammed his fist on my desk and exclaimed, "Why didn't they put something in the gas to make it smell bad? That's supposed to be in the gas to warn people of a gas leak. Who was responsible for providing heat? I want answers."

On October 7, freshmen Rosa Rosati and Barbara Breen, tired of growing up feeling guilty, admitting, confessing, apologizing and obeying, joined a group of Catholic students who were traveling from Stedman University, a Jesuit college, to Wichita, Kansas, a few hours away from campus, to attend a Jehovah's Witness religious retreat and explore converting. They returned to their off-campus apartment late Sunday evening. The weather had turned cold. They turned on a wall heater in their bathroom and went to bed.

When Rosa and Barbara didn't show up for Monday morning classes or by a noontime prayer session, Dawn Flood, who had been on the trip and who knew that Rosa had been feeling feverish, thought they might be sick. When nobody answered the doorbell at their apartment, Dawn opened the door. An awful smell smacked her face. Heat was coming from the bathroom. Rosa was asleep in her bed, so Dawn pulled the covers off her face and whispered in her ear. No response. She shook her. Still no response. She pulled Rosa's hand from beneath the covers and discovered that her fingers were cold and turning blue. In the other bed, Barbara lay under the covers. Dawn pulled the covers off Barbara's face and then, petrified, ran as fast as she could down the stairway and four blocks to the Dean's Office.

Rosa was dead. Barbara was in a coma.

I knew it would be expensive to investigate and prosecute a case involving a defective heater, especially one in far away Enid, Oklahoma, where Stedman was located. What made matters worse was that I also knew that the death of a child did not command large jury verdicts. Callous as it may seem, I explained that a parent was not entitled to money for emotional distress, but only for monetary loss. Since Rosa was a college student, not working and contributing to the family, there was no monetary damage. Their only claim was for the guidance, counsel and affection that they would expect to receive from Rosa when they were elderly.

"You mean someone pays less if they kill someone instead of just injuring them?" Anne, Rosa's mother, disappointed and astounded, drew a section of her lower lip between her teeth and slowly released it. "Gee," she said. "I don't agree with the law. But unfortunately, that's the way it is."

Rosa's father's head wobbled and his hands shook.

"The law is archaic and out of touch because it comes from England, where no one could sue the king. When one of the king's men ran over a boy in a procession, the public outcry was so loud that the king permitted a lawsuit, but he limited damages to the actual monetary loss the parents suffered, namely the funeral expense. Our law hasn't kept up with modern times," I said.

When Rosa's father and mother left, they appeared much calmer than when they had arrived and I felt I had fulfilled my duty to give them forthright professional advice. But I couldn't concentrate. Was I behaving like Mr. Mustache? I remembered how other families we met at the New York University's Rusk Rehabilitation Institute hospital after Ellen's and Jared's injuries felt about lawyers. My father was conservative, had survived the Depression and was risk averse. Experienced lawyers in Trenton often told me that the life of a lawyer was a marathon, not a sprint. With risk came big wins, but also big losses. Slow and steady was the route to success.

I was compelled to reach out to someone in Enid. Enid Detective Donald Jones told me that the District Attorney investigated and that the case was closed. He did not think anyone would be willing to take on the gas company on behalf of a student who died since, even on its best day, the case was only worth from ten to twenty thousand dollars. Besides, the students' landlord was a university, to which anyone who was anyone in town was connected.

Hamilton James, an Enid lawyer listed in Martindale-Hubbell, a reputable lawyer's directory, contacted a construction and premises liability expert at my request. In spite of what Rosa's father had said there was no defect in the heater because there was no requirement that a gas company put an odorant in the gas used in a heater. That seemed to be the central theory of fault in the case.

"What about a case against the landlord?" I inquired.

"What's the address again? East Randolph, is it?"

"Yes, 210."

"That row of houses has been there for at least a hundred years. The university owns them. You'll have a big problem bringing a case against them—you'd have to prove the landlord knew about a defect in order to hold him responsible. I'm sure no one else had the same problem or they'd be poisoned too," James said.

Rosa's father insisted I go to Enid and find out more, advancing the money for two airplane tickets and a hotel. I had learned while representing a seriously injured person in South Jersey a few years before that a case like the one Rosa's father wanted me to investigate was too much for one person. A team was required to deal with the stress a person and family experience in navigating the morass of legal, medical and social problems involved. Legal assistants were the "ears" who listened to clients when we lawyers were giving our undivided attention to preparing for and trying cases.

Billboards heralding "Jesus Saves" welcomed my partner David Botwinick and me as we drove from Oklahoma City to Enid through flatland dotted with oilrigs and passed dark fields, which now supported empty grain elevators. It was a few hours before dusk when we pulled into a space behind a pickup truck, a shotgun resting on a rack in its rear window, parked in front of the No Name Bar on a shady downtown university square. We looked around at a luncheonette, a five-and-dime, a clothing store, pawnshop and six bars. I pulled a briefcase from the back seat, rested it on the trunk and pulled out a slip of paper. David loaded a Polaroid camera with film.

A man wearing a red and black wool shirt ambled out of the No Name Bar and tossed a cigarette into the gutter.

"Where's 210 East Randolph?"

He pointed across the square.

The front door of the three-story brick walkup was open. We climbed a dimly lit flight of steps to Rosa and Barbara's apartment. If the door was locked, where would we get a key? David read my mind. "Let's give it a try," he said.

I turned the doorknob and pushed. The door creaked open. A flick of a light switch turned on an exposed incandescent bulb that illuminated a small hallway leading to a bedroom on the left and to a kitchen on the right. David removed a "Rules of Occupancy for University Students" placard from the door and put it in his briefcase. In the bedroom, the bed covers had been removed from two beds, but the sheets were still in place, eerily unwrinkled. The bed covers were neatly folded and piled under the single window on the far wall. David took pictures, pulled the film from the camera and placed it on the bed to develop.

When I turned the knob on the wall heater in the bathroom, yellow flames jumped up. Just what Rosa's father had said would happen if the heater wasn't working properly. David photographed the flames then moved closer and took a shot of soot marks on the heater's enamel cover. He slid his finger over the cover again. "Soot should not have been there if the heater was working properly. Clean burning gas shouldn't leave soot." I knew that from my experience with my outdoor gas grill. He rubbed his thumb where he had already wiped his finger. Because there was no old, hard soot beneath the fresh soot, he suspected the problem was relatively recent.

Since it was necessary to show a landlord or the gas company had notice of a dangerous condition in order to make them responsible, we left the apartment thinking there was no case. To me, the law was unfair but I didn't know anything else to do but accept it.

The next morning, we met Barbara's parents at Mercy Hospital and told them that we were in Enid because Rosa's father thought there was a possibility that the university and the gas company had something to do with what had happened.

"Right now," Barbara's father said, "all we're concerned about is our daughter."

On the flight home that evening, David and I examined the photographs we had taken. "Look at the flames," David said peremptorily. "They're yellow. Even the gas grill at my apartment has a label warning against cooking inside if the flame is not clear blue. A yellow flame means the gas is giving off carbon monoxide."

Flipping through the pictures, David pointed out the blankets. "There are a lot of them. Damn it. It was cold in the apartment, so what did they do? They lit the gas heater and went to sleep all bundled up. The apartment filled up with deadly gas."

In our law library the next morning, we researched the responsibility of a university to a student who lived in an off-campus apartment. Landlord-tenant law required proof that the landlord-university had notice of a dangerous condition. It had no duty to inspect the premises to find a defect, as it would have if it were a business. Since we could not prove that the landlord-university or the gas company had notice, there was no case.

I fiddled with my thumbs. A judge would throw this case out. I called Rosa's parents, relieved that I had fulfilled my professional responsibility and thinking that would be the last time that I would speak with them.

A month later, when Father Armand, their parish priest, called me to help another parishioner he reported that Rosa's parents were not doing well. "They can't accept that no one is responsible for Rosa's death. The law is so unfair."

Father Armand had referred other parishioners to me because he appreciated my lending a free legal ear to his flock. "I'll give it another look," I said before asking, "How's the girl in the coma doing?" I wondered if she was still living. Karen Quinlan, a New Jersey girl, had garnered a lot of ink because she lay in a coma, brain-dead, on a respirator because her Catholic parents did not want her to die. Barbara had come out of the coma and was at a rehabilitation center in Columbus, Ohio, fifty miles from her home.

I sat there thinking that the university should have been required to inspect a student apartment. Why wasn't the university considered a business, not a landlord? Rosa's father and mother paid for her to go to Stedman. A business has the duty to warn potential customers about any defects on the property. Was I courting danger, getting bogged down in an unprofitable case that would make it impossible to take on the next good one that came along?

A week later, a young woman in her twenties straightened her legs and stood as I entered the waiting room of my office. Two black metal suitcases rested on the gray, tweed carpet beside her feet. She introduced herself as Alice Englehart, who was demonstrating a new product called Lexis.

"What reference books do you have in your library?" she asked.

"The New Jersey and Federal," I said nonchalantly, referring to the volumes of law books most law firms owned.

"Lexis is a new computerized method of doing legal research. With it you can get cases from all fifty states. Would you like a demonstration?" I agreed. She set up her computer and printer on a table.

"What would you like me to look up?"

"How about 'university student dies from carbon monoxide poisoning in student apartment'."

"Let's try 'student' and 'housing' first. It's the broadest search. We can narrow it down after if we have to."

She typed "student/housing" on her computer. Cases popped up on the screen. "Let's add 'injured.'" She scanned the screen. "Here are two cases. Let's bring them up." She pushed a few more keys.

"Devin versus Andover Academy – it's a Massachusetts case. Let's see what it says."

Line by line, the case came out of her printer. On the first page, the synopsis stated: "The case holds a preparatory school responsible for a student's injury in a dormitory because the school was a business. The school exercised complete control over the premises and, therefore, owed the student a duty to inspect and to warn of dangerous conditions that could have been discovered by a reasonably prudent person."

My heart skipped a beat.

"Any more cases like that?"

"Here's one in Alaska. Let's try it."

The case flashed on the screen.

"Same thing. Private school. Injury. Decides that a school is a business. There's something more here... "

I craned my neck over her shoulder. Words appeared on the screen: "In order to raise the duty of a school from a landlord to a business, a plaintiff has the burden of proving by a preponderance of the believable evidence that the school administration exhibited the same or similar level of control over the premises that a business owner does or should exhibit over the premises where the plaintiff suffered injury or harm."

Typewriters had gone from manual to electric, then automatic, and the Xerox machine had replaced carbon paper. Now cases from all over the country could be printed out at the push of a button. How long would it be before law firm libraries would be memories? New technology had given me an excellent competitive advantage.

"Look at these." I slid the Lexis printouts in front of David.

After skimming the case summaries, he looked up, his pupils as big as eight balls. "We've got a shot," he said.

"We may have a case against the university," I told Rosa's parents.

"The university?"

"I found some cases that might get us around the law that prevents bringing a case against the university. The bad news is that the courts are pretty conservative. I'd probably lose in the trial court and have to appeal. The appellate court is more liberal. But to be successful, we would be asking the court to make new law based on cases in other states.

"Have you told Barbara's folks?" Rosa's mother asked.

"No."

"Maybe you should. They don't want to relive something that is so hurtful, just to lose. That's like dying twice. But if there's a chance of winning, they may want to take it."

Richard and Mary, Barbara's parents, met me at ten o'clock the next Saturday at a hotel in Columbus. They were upset, very upset.

"The university is claiming the girls committed suicide," Barbara's father said. "They're saying the girls were unhappy. Born Catholics, Rosa and Barbara were thinking of converting to Jehovah's Witnesses. The Dean of Students was very upset. He is saying the girls didn't fit in and that the carbon monoxide poisoning was intentional. Worse yet, he is saying they took their own lives, fearing that telling their parents would ruin their lives, our lives."

Barbara's mother's nape flushed. "We took out a medical insurance policy on Barbara. Not much. Just fifty thousand. The insurance company has written us that if Barbara dies they will not pay until they investigate what the university is claiming. If Barbara tried to commit suicide, they don't have to pay us."

Barbara's father his face red, took a deep, exhausted breath. "We'd like you to help us if you think you can."

I did not believe for a minute that the girls tried to hurt themselves. There was no note. If there was no history of depression or other evidence common to suicide cases, I didn't think it would be difficult to get the fifty thousand from the medical insurance because the insurance company would have a difficult time proving a suicide attempt.

I immediately telephoned David and told him David about the suicide claim. He was livid. "That's bullshit," he raved.

"It may be bullshit, but it's another factor we have to consider."

"This claim stinks. I smell a fucking rat," David ranted.

"The good news is Barbara is likely to survive. If her brain damage is permanent, this is a big case. The bad news is we have a bad case. But at least our fee on the insurance case will help defray some of our investigation expenses."

"If we can't get the court to accept the Alaska and Massachusetts cases, ours will be tossed out."

"Agreed," I said. "If the case is thrown out on legal grounds, the expenses will be limited. If the judge recognizes the Alaska and Massachusetts cases, we have a shot at a good settlement. A big jury verdict would be even better. We need evidence that supports the theory that the university is a business, that the furnace was not on, and that the girls turned on the bathroom heater to get warm. We need Barbara, who is competent and who remembers what happened."

That's when I called Doctor Herbert Spiegel, the doctor in charge of Barbara's treatment.

"Right now," he said, "Barbara can't talk. She can blink her eyes. She can hear but can understand only a few things. We know that because she responds to simple commands, like open your eyes or lift your head, but we don't know what she will be able to do, if anything, in the future."

Three months later, Doctor Spiegel ushered me into Barbara's room. Her pale and wan face still showed the good looks of a university prom queen. She stared blankly while I held her hand.

"Can I ask her some questions? Like 'did she go to the cellar to check the heater'?'"

"I don't think she can remember something like that. She's only able to recall a state of mind, not actual facts. Maybe sometime in the future. Maybe in six months. Who knows?"

Barbara made slow but steady progress. She walked on parallel bars and talked haltingly in a slow monotone. She was able to verify our theory of what had happened, with two exceptions. She and Rosa did not check the heater in the basement because the door to the basement was locked. They called the Building and Grounds Department to report how cold the apartment was and were told the problem would be resolved in the morning.

Doctor Spiegel explained how Barbara could remember events that happened more than a year ago but forget information that I had told her minutes before. "There's a difference between short-term and long-term memory. Most people can't understand why it happens. Some people remember things that happened in their childhood but can't recognize the person they are talking to." I had some knowledge of brain injury that occurred when someone struck his or her head on a solid surface from another case and books I had read, but knew very little about how a gas like carbon monoxide could affect memory. I paid rapt attention to Spiegel as he explained how the gas deprived brain cells of the oxygen they needed to live. "I'll get some books for you. There's a lot of new research being done in the field of brain neurology," he explained.

Barbara' case became an obsession. Literature dealt mainly with traumatic brain injuries. I read everything I could about brain injuries. There wasn't a lot written about what happened to victims of carbon monoxide poisoning because most people did not survive.

I traveled to Enid to meet with the premises liability expert with whom Hamilton James had spoken. He examined my photographs and visited the apartment. He told me that the gas company had never inspected the bathroom heater because it did not have a "red tag," and that the heater was illegally hooked up to a kitchen line. A search at the Enid town hall did not turn up any permit obtained by the university.

After I started a lawsuit alleging that the university's negligence killed Rosa and injured Barbara, John Webster, an Oklahoma City lawyer who had earned a national reputation as a defense lawyer, filed papers on behalf of the university, asserting that the university was a landlord, that it had no prior notice of a defect in the gas heater, and therefore, such a frivolous claim should not take up precious court time.

Two months later, John Webster sat on a plush leather sofa outside Judge Delaney's chambers at nine in the morning. In a deep voice he said, "Better we get rid of this case sooner rather than later." I felt a violent, excruciating pain in my chest.

Judge Delaney's court clerk ushered us into his chambers. The judge, in short sleeves, sitting at the head of an oval conference table, rose as we entered.

"Web, you're here again?" Judge Delaney began.

Webster turned to me and smiled insidiously.

Delaney took off a pair of half moon spectacles and put his thumb and forefinger on the bridge of his nose. Grey eyes floated from Webster and then to me. Judge Delaney told me he thought that the law of landlord and tenant controlled the case, but that after he had read my brief arguing that business law that required the university to inspect the heater for defects applied, he had second thoughts. I breathed a sigh of relief. Judge Delaney clasped his hands in a prayer position waiting for Webster's response.

"The university would have to have exclusive control of the premises. In this case, the girls had complete control. They had a kitchen, they cleaned the apartment on their own, and lived just like any other tenants," Webster argued.

Judge Delaney rubbed his chin and leaned forward. "Here's what I'm going to do." He eyed me. "You have sixty days to take a sworn statement of any three people from the university at a deposition. If you can't prove exclusive control, the case is over."

The court rules provided that a party to a lawsuit could take sworn oral statements from witnesses. The procedure called a deposition is carried out at a place convenient to the opposing party, usually in a lawyer's office. The testimony given has the same force and effect as if given in a courtroom.

David and I decided to take sworn statements from Dean James Bernard, Dean of Students, Charles Percel, the head of Building and Grounds, and Joel Hodges, the supervisor of dormitory maintenance, the person responsible for the inspections of university properties.

John Webster decided we should take depositions in Dean James Bernard's office. Webster introduced me to Charles Percel, a heavyset man with a round face, bulbous eyes and a wide nose. His midsection was huge and when he sat down, his plaid shirttail pulled out of his green work pants.

Percel testified he had been in charge of the university dormitories for twenty-six years. He was the only person responsible for turning on the heat in the dormitories. Rules and regulations that governed what a student could do with the dormitory heat were on a placard that he posted on the dorm room doors. The placard told students "not to mess with the thermostats and if there's a problem to call." After admitting that when he found out that that a cold front was coming through on October 7, he turned on the furnaces in the dormitories, Percel raised his eyebrows toward the ceiling and looked over at poker-faced John Webster. Nothing in the Rules and Regulations told the girls to call the gas company to turn on the furnace. Percel didn't know who was responsible to call the gas company to turn heat on in an off campus apartment. He thought it was up to the gas company.

"I'd like Mr. Bernard next," I said to Webster.

James Bernard, the Dean of Students, stared at me and pressed his hands against the edge of the table. Bernard was responsible for putting placards on the doors of student housing units to instruct and warn of any problems. He made the rules and saw to it that they were enforced. He did not think that a placard 'Rules and Regulations' was posted on the back door of the apartment occupied by Barbara and Rosa. A month or so afterward, he had gone to the apartment and looked for it. It wasn't there.

Dean Bernard had gone to the apartment after David and me.

"Are the 'Rules and Regulations' safety rules?"

"Yes."

"So you are responsible for the safety of students at the university?"

"Unfortunately," he said.

Bernard asserted that Joel Hodges was in charge of inspecting the furnaces in the dormitories, but that the gas company was responsible for turning the heaters in student apartments on and off.

"Who is responsible for calling the gas company to turn the heating on or off?" I asked.

"Building and Grounds."

Having gotten the answer I wanted, I switched my line of questioning.

"Rosa and Barbara sought counseling prior to October 7, didn't they?"

According to the records, they were homesick and had some problems adjusting here, not something that was uncommon for freshmen. No medications had been prescribed for Rosa or Barbara.

What was that about medications?" David asked in the hallway during the break we took before questioning Joel Hodges.

"I'll explain later. Let's go nail down Hodges."

"You better because Bernard opened the door you closed with Percel."

"What do you mean?" I inquired.

"Didn't you hear him say that the gas company had authority to turn on the furnace? You didn't ask about inspection authority. There may have been joint authority between the university and the gas company," David warned.

"Good point. Thanks," I said.

Joel Hodges shifted in his chair. Beads of sweat formed on his forehead. Fingering the glass table, he left marks. It was his responsibility to call the gas company to turn on the furnace at 210 East Randolph. Percel was his supervisor. He knew to call "when Charlie tells me." Percel had not told him to call the gas company to turn on the heat before the girls arrived home from Wichita. Charlie told him to call the gas company "right after they took out the girls." He was at the apartment when the ambulances took out the girls. It was steaming and it "stunk like a skunk." It took the gas company only an hour to come and turn on the furnace. There were no tags on the bathroom heater, indicating that the gas company had never inspected the bathroom heater. The heater was illegally hooked up to a kitchen line so the university never got a permit.

With no permit issued, the gas company would not know about the bathroom heater. Stedman had exclusive control of Rosa and Barbara's apartment.

"So you think you're going to clean my clock?" John Webster asked when I appeared at the courthouse to begin the trial.

I had learned what to expect from Webster. "I don't know if I'm going to clean your clock but it's high noon on the prairie," I replied.

"Wait until you see a university town jury," Webster continued.

"I know what you're saying."

"You do, do ya?"

"You might dress like them. But I'll talk like them from my heart. I have you cold turkey on liability. Judge Delaney is going to charge the jury that the university is a business, that it had exclusive control of the apartment and duty to inspect the bathroom heater. The damages are horrendous. A million and a half would not be unreasonable."

Webster was taken aback with my brash confidence "If he charges business law, you're buying an appeal. You'll wait for your money until hell freezes over. I'm sure you've told your clients about appeals."

"I sure have." That wasn't true. Barbara's father and mother wanted me to try to settle for four hundred thousand and Rosa's parents would be satisfied with forty thousand. The journey to court had been exhausting. They were strangers to the Bible belt, worried that a jury would not be sympathetic to Stedman and prejudiced toward Catholic girls who were rebelling against their religion.

"Four hundred fifty's been the highest verdict ever in this state for someone who can walk and talk. Barbara can walk and talk. You know brain injured people who make a recovery like her are hard to understand. She looks good; so what if her speech is impaired and she limps? That's not worth close to a million. And what is the jury going to think when I ask about her childhood and high school and she remembers everything?"

"But her memory is impaired. She can't hold down a job."

"You argue that and then tell the jury she remembers everything she did on October 7, two years ago, and let's see how the jury takes it. You can't have it both ways," Webster snapped. "Are your folks interested in talking settlement?"

"It depends on the terms."

"What you're asking isn't fair. A million and a half is something you're only going to get from the jury," Webster quipped.

"We're here and ready to proceed," I countered.

"As is the university," Webster replied, wheeling around and walking away.

I had learned that representing any traumatically injured person requires a lot of energy. The obstacles that seriously injured face are immense. Their battles are uphill ones. I had been confronted with making difficult choices, torn between carrying out a client's wishes to the letter and doing what I knew would be better for the client in the long run. Sometimes I had to make decisions that upset people, like tying up money in a trust or a structured settlement annuity to prevent it from being squandered. Negotiating with my own client created a dilemma: do I make the smart choice or take the easy way out and give in to the immediate desire of my client?

The verbal jockeying continued in the hallway until the court clerk informed us that Judge Delaney wanted to see us in chambers. This time the judge was at his desk.

"Gentlemen, I'm prepared to pick a jury. Are your clients interested in a settlement?"

"They are if the offer is fair."

"A good settlement is one where both parties are unhappy."

"That's not my definition, Your Honor," Webster snapped.

"I know it's not, Web. You never know what a jury will do." Judge Delaney's eyes glanced furtively at me. "A bird in hand is often worth two in the bush."

"Your Honor, I'm prepared to offer one hundred thousand dollars. Twenty-five to the Rosa's parents and seventy-five to Barbara," Webster stated, matter-of-factly.

"That's a good start. I'm sure you're prepared to offer more, aren't you?"

"Judge, I have a little more, but not much more."

"What is your response to that?"

"Your Honor, I would reject the offer outright. I have to communicate it to my clients, but I know what they will say." I had learned that defense lawyers often offer substantially less than they are authorized because they know a plaintiff's lawyer must communicate every offer to his client.

"Go and talk to them," Judge Delaney insisted.

In a conference room, Barbara's father called the offers "an insult." Rosa's parents agreed. I told them I believed Webster was making a low offer, trying to feel them out.

"When I reject the offer, I think Webster will try to raise the offer on Rosa's case and then try to settle Barbara's for about two hundred thousand. I agree we should turn the offers down. I had experienced similar procedures with judges and defense lawyers, but never with the stakes so high.

"At least they're admitting they're at fault," Rosa's father said.

"I'm sure they're going to try to bring the suicide claim up one way or another," Barbara's mother added. "Catholics don't believe in it."

"I don't think they'll have a leg to stand on. Dean Bernard admitted that even though the girls were homesick, they weren't so depressed that they needed any medication. I'm not worried."

"So what's next?" Barbara asked, her voice shaky. It was the first time today she had spoken and I hadn't realized she understood what was going on.

"I will tell the judge we reject the offers. Then he will meet with one side and the other, trying to get us closer together."

Barbara stared into space, mute.

It is difficult to know when to accept a settlement. It's like playing chess, with pitfalls in almost every move. Nothing would bring Rosa back, but money could change the way Barbara lived in the future.

When Webster and I entered chambers, Judge Delaney was fiddling with a pen.

"What was your client's response?" he asked curtly.

"They were insulted, Your Honor."

"You do know, don't you, that the death case on a good day can't be worth more than fifty."

"Your Honor, fifty will not settle this case."

"Why not?"

"Because if I try it with Barbara's case, it is worth more money. A jury's going to give Barbara more than a million. When they compare her to Rosa, they're going to go high on Barbara. If they give Rosa fifty, they have to award Barbara at least ten times that. She is going to live with her pain and disability for many years."

"That's what you think," Judge Delaney remarked. "But couldn't the jury, following my instructions, give Rosa's parents twenty-five and then say to themselves, 'Well, if a death is worth twenty-five, then an injury like Barbara's is only worth a hundred.'"

I don't think so, Your Honor. At any rate, my clients are willing to let a jury tell them that, rather than settle. They're willing to take the risk."

"You know a jury verdict will be appealed."

"I've explained that to them. They're adults."

"Web, why don't you excuse yourself?" Judge Delaney asked.

Webster stood and followed the judge's instruction.

We went back and forth, in and out of Judge Delaney's chambers, sometimes meeting with him alone and sometimes together. When I was alone with Judge Delaney, he kept emphasizing how horrible it would be for Barbara to walk out of the courthouse with nothing. He tried to befriend me by telling me he would try to get Web to "raise the ante." By noon, Webster had offered forty thousand dollars to Rosa's parents and one hundred fifty thousand to Barbara. I assumed John Webster had authority to pay two hundred thousand and was saving some ammunition for later.

At twelve-thirty, Judge Delaney recessed for lunch. We wound our way back to the Joyce Kilmer Hotel. I sensed that the acknowledgment of guilt was what was important to Rosa's father and mother and that they were ready to settle. Rosa's mother said to Barbara, "We would be satisfied with the offer, but we don't want to let you down. We wouldn't be here if it weren't for you joining in this case." Barbara's mother took Rosa's mother's hand. "But you have to do what is right for you. Barbara feels badly that she is here and Rosa is not."

Over lunch, I tried to keep discussion of the settlement at a minimum since I could see my clients were becoming impatient. David helped keep things light by joking about John Webster's cordovan shoes, and orange and black tie, and my worn, brown shoes and red and blue tie. The shoes were my lucky trial shoes, which I wore with every color suit, whether it was black, blue, brown, gray, or green. I had won seven cases in a row since I had bought them.

I lost three in a row wearing contact lenses. I abandoned them.

When we resumed after lunch, I told Judge Delaney that "one hundred will do it for Rosa's parents, a million for Barbara."

"There's an old saying: 'The only way you get a million dollar verdict is if the defense makes no offer and your case is worth three million.' Are you ready to pick a jury?" Judge Delaney asked, his voice rising.

"If forty and a hundred and fifty is the final offer?" I replied. The temperature in the court was rising. I hoped the offer would, too.

"Web, give us a minute together," Judge Delaney said.

Webster stepped out.

"I've had a chance to talk to Mr. Webster," Judge Delaney began, consolingly. "I told him to call his insurance company and tell them that one fifty isn't going to do it. Let's wait and see what he says before we pick a jury."

The judge had become part of the negotiations. He wanted to complete them and avoid an appeal, which would mean having his rulings attacked by Webster or by me.

Barbara's mother and father had decided to let the jury decide Barbara's case unless Stedman paid Barbara four hundred thousand so that she could net a quarter of a million dollars, which they would invest at seven per cent. At their insistence, I reduced my demand from a million dollars to seven hundred fifty thousand. By day's end, I had received offers of forty thousand dollars for Rosa's case and two hundred fifty thousand dollars for Barbara's.

I invited everyone to an early dinner. Both families told me they wanted to be alone. I wanted to be with them, because I was afraid they would decide to accept the offers, and I wanted to discourage them. They insisted on being by themselves. David and I went out for dinner alone.

The opening statement, which I had rehearsed the night before, played over and over in my head. When I got to the courthouse the next day, John Webster paced the hallway. "I can't believe what's happening," he said. "My insurance company called me at home last night. They want to pay the sixty thousand dollars on Rosa's case. I can't believe it. But I'm under an obligation to offer the money to you. I disagree with their position, but so it is. It's theirs to accept. There won't be another nickel."

"What about Barbara?"

"I'm afraid they're done."

"I'll relay the offer and let you know," I said, caught by surprise.

Shortly before nine, Rosa's mother and father got off the elevator. I led them to a conference room where I conveyed Webster's offer.

They both said, "Let's take it."

My Adams apple rolled in my throat. My eyes shut and I inhaled. "I would love you to hang in there with Barbara. I know you have your own rights, but I think if we stick together we can help her."

"Can the insurance company withdraw the offer?" Rosa's father asked.

" I can't guarantee it won't, but it's rarely done."

Rosa's father asked to be left alone with his wife and I went into the hallway. Webster caught my eye. He opened his arms and mouthed, "Okay?"

I shrugged my shoulders and pointed to the conference room, indicating that Rosa's mother and father were talking.

The conference room door opened and Rosa's father beckoned me. The door shut behind me. They told me they would follow my advice.

I walked over to Webster, standing in a corner at the end of the hallway. "They want seventy-five thousand."

"Where do they think they are, Las Vegas?"

"They think they're going to win. You ever work with a stubborn client?"

"They ever see a stubborn lawyer?"

"They're sticking with Barbara. They don't care about money at this point." I would never know whether John Webster realized I was not telling him the truth.

Judge Delaney had other matters that he had to hear and decide, and instructed us to return at one-thirty.

After lunch, while waiting in the conference room, Barbara told us, in a halting staccato, that she was edgy about the chances of losing, her mom and dad going into debt if she lost, and afraid she would clam up on the witness stand. Tears filled her eyes and rolled down her cheeks. I told everyone to take Barbara to the hotel and not to come back to the courthouse until I called them.

At one-thirty sharp, the judge's clerk called both attorneys into chambers. Judge Delaney was sitting in his high back chair. Webster said his company was willing to pay sixty thousand to settle Rosa's case. Judge Delaney was sure that would satisfy them. I said I had had instructions to accept no less than seventy-five thousand.

"Web, what do you have on Barbara?"

"Nothing more there, Your Honor," Webster replied.

"Web, let's talk," Judge Delaney ordered.

After five minutes, I was invited back.

"Here's where we are," Judge Delaney began. "You have a very seriously injured young lady. I believe she is an innocent person. You've done a yeoman's job getting this far. Don't press your luck. I have recommended to Mr. Webster that he get seventy-five for Rosa and four and a quarter for Barbara, for a total of a half million. Mr. Webster is going to the telephone and I would like to talk to your clients."

"Your Honor, that's not fair. To pressure them is not appropriate," I replied anxiously, knowing that my clients would accept the offer.

"As you like it," Judge Delaney said.

A long half an hour passed. Judge Delaney, wearing his robe, came out of his chambers and sauntered to the bench on which I was seated. "Mr. Webster has come back with some good news. He has sixty-five thousand dollars on Rosa's case and four hundred ten thousand for Barbara. One more thing. Stedman insists that any settlement be kept confidential. Secret."

I knew immediately that he had the seventy-five and four and a quarter.

I called the hotel. I prodded Rosa's mother and father to stick with Barbara, and they reluctantly agreed with the proviso that if the case didn't settle by the end of the day, they were going to accept the offer. An additional ten thousand would not make much difference to them, and they did not want to risk either a jury trial or alienating the judge. I told Barbara's mother and father that if we got the case to the jury, Webster would come up with seven hundred fifty thousand.

Stedman did not want publicity. They didn't want the case to go before a jury, exposing its crass violation of the law, having an illegal heater in a freshman's apartment.

Just before four-thirty, John Webster asked me to come into the judge's chambers. "I have been instructed to tell you that if Barbara will accept five hundred thousand dollars, the claims manager will call New York, where the main office is located, and recommend it. I can't assure you he'll get it, but I have every reason to believe he can."

"What do you say?" Judge Delaney inquired.

"Let me talk to my clients," I said, smiling at the judge to show that I appreciated what he was doing.

He returned the smile.

Webster gave me his telephone number, telling me to call him after I spoke with my clients.

At the hotel, I explained to Barbara and her parents that I thought Mr. Webster had authority to pay five hundred thousand. I told them if they said they would accept it, he would offer less. Barbara's father understood what I was saying and agreed to let me negotiate. We agreed that if the insurance company did not offer five hundred, then we would tell Rosa's mother and father to settle and go to trial alone.

Barbara sobbed. The heat was getting to her. She wanted to get on with her life, whatever it was going to be. All the money in the world would not make up for what she had gone through.

I called Webster. "We are stuck at seven fifty."

"Dammit, I don't usually cave in like this, but there's five hundred thousand on the table. Take it or leave it." The heat had gotten to John Webster, too.

The case was settled.

The next morning, Judge Delaney said, his tone now filled with satisfaction, "I want to make sure Barbara understands the terms. If not, I may have to appoint a guardian to make sure her interests are protected." Judge Delaney stood, his eyes looking down at me. "I was not going to charge the jury that the university is a business." Webster's shoulders slumped over and his chin dropped to his chest.

At our celebration dinner, Rosa's mother said she wanted to set up a scholarship fund so other youngsters at Rosa's high school could get the college education Rosa didn't get, Rosa's father confided. "The toughest thing is that during this case it was as though my daughter was still alive. Now she's gone. I know I fought for her. And so did you fellows," At that moment, I realized that Rosa's mother and father would not have risked a trial because they did not want to experience Rosa's dying twice. I could only imagine what it would be like for them if a jury returned to the courtroom and declared them losers. It had happened in less serious cases I had tried, and I knew the anger that the losing client felt toward the judicial system and their lawyer.

In an oak-paneled courtroom Judge Charles Delaney spoke to Barbara, "The half-million dollar settlement you have received is the largest in the history of this state. Mr. and Mrs. Rosati, the seventy-five thousand dollars you are being paid by the university is the most any parents have ever been paid in this state for the death of a child."

The morning after the settlement I was exhausted, somber, and unhappy when an American Airlines 707 lifted off from Oklahoma City's Will Rogers Airport into a setting sun. At four o'clock just one morning ago, in a strange hotel I wondered why I had taken a case so far away, and questioned if I would physically make it to court. If only I had tried the case and gotten a jury verdict like I did for Angelo and Terry. If only I had not agreed to John Webster's demand that the settlement be kept secret. Other victims would have to take difficult risks to get justice for themselves and others.

Fiddling with my fingers, I had impatiently shifted back and forth in my airplane seat while I downed a few scotches. A winter snowstorm blanketed the Great Plains. The pilot announced that Chicago's O'Hare Airport was closed, to expect turbulence, and to be patient because the flight would be at least two hours late. The pilot had to fly in a holding pattern before being cleared for landing in Milwaukee.

Suddenly the airplane rollercoastered in the sky. A few minutes later, a man sporting a railroad worker's cap and a black and white striped shirt, wobbled down the aisle, grabbing one seat back after another, bellowing, "I'm Casey Jones. You'd have gotten home faster if you had taken the train." As Casey passed me, I broke into a smile when I noticed the tail of a pilot's jacket protruding from beneath his striped shirt.

I questioned the advice a veteran trial had given me when I discussed the case with him before I had gone to Oklahoma. "The best-tried case is a settled case," he said because it saved the client from the stresses and uncertainties of the legal system and brought a case to an end. I had put so much effort into the case that I had convinced myself I was going to win a large jury verdict.

I was sitting at my desk after a hectic day at the Trenton courthouse. Why, I asked myself, was I so unfulfilled and moody a month after a settlement that I should have been proud of? I questioned whether I was too weak to withstand the rigors and pressures placed upon me by our court system. I had desperately wanted to change the law so that others wouldn't suffer the fate Rosa and Barbara had.

A defense lawyer known for paying injured plaintiffs as little as he could, was eating lunch by himself at a restaurant across the street from my office. After I asked if I could join him, he listened while I told him what was bothering me about the settlement I made in Oklahoma.

"Our profession is an art, not a science. The system's not perfect by a long shot. But it's the best that man has devised," he said. He tilted his head a bit and leaned forward. "Look here, Albert. You've had some good luck. You did okay out there in Oklahoma, where none of us would have dared to tread. Good lawyers are like Sherlock Holmes. Always trying to figure something out, putting the pieces of the puzzle together. Life in the law is a never ending search—not always for justice, and not always for money."

I received an envelope from Mutual of Omaha Insurance Company. In it was a letter that said that they had completed their investigation into the case of

Barbara Breen. Enclosed was the settlement.

My mood began to improve. The case did bring enough money to bring things into Barbara's life that could compensate for much of what she had lost.

Six months after the settlement, David poked his head in the door and asked his usual question, "What's up?"

Hamilton James called, "The premises liability expert told him that the gas company was putting an odorous agent in their gas. What happened to Barbara and Rosa would not happen again."

At the time of the settlement, the finest brain injury doctor in the nation told me that Barbara would never be able to work or live independently. He believed that Barbara's family, even with the best of intentions, could not take care of her for long, that families on average, only put up with the stress for about three years before abandoning their brain-injured relatives to group homes or long-term care facilities.

Barbara was living with her parents, who were focused not only on Barbara, but on her case against the University. Richard Breen established a trust with the funds Barbara received.at a local bank. So far so good. Barbara was in good hands.

Barbara did not end up staying with her parents for very long. She met a man, who became her boyfriend. He convinced her to move in with him in Arizona. Richard Breen died suddenly and Mary became her trustee. Mary peeved that Barbara ignored her advice let Barbara permit the boyfriend to fleece her out of almost one hundred thousand dollars. "I hope she learned a lesson," Mary once told me when she called me to counsel Barbara.

Barbara and her family decided it would be for the best if she moved back to Mary's home. Where else would she go? Barbara was unwilling to confine herself in the kind of environment where staff attended to brain-injured patients. She valued her autonomy for that. Barbara could not live independently or with a roommate.

Barbara returned home with Mary, who, unbeknownst to me, was her step mother. Mary distanced herself from Barbara, while using some of Barbara's money for "their support."

Ken happened to go to Barbara's tenth high school reunion where he met her for the first time since high school. Ken and Barbara had been high school friends. Barbara was always dressed to the nines. She was wearing a beautiful black dress, but walked funny. Ken thought that maybe she was in a car accident. They struck up a conversation. Her speech was very slow and monotone from the brain injury that she suffered. They ended up keeping in touch and struck up a friendship. Barbara didn't want to live with Mary anymore. Discussing her feelings with me, Mary said, "It is very hard for her to see me the way I am. She is constantly stressed and frustrated."

After Ken heard about the situation, he thought about it for a long time. Ken invited her to stay with him for a few weeks.

Finally, he decided that he had to let her move in with him in Ft. Lauderdale, Florida. In Barbara's condition, she was unable to live by herself. Ken was determined to at least give it a try living with Barbara. Ken understood Mary's feelings, that you can love a person to death, but if you can't handle it you walk away. "Not everyone is cut out to take care of a brain-injured person," he told her. Ken did not even ask her to pay for rent, food and the phone bill.

My telephone rang constantly, so it seemed. The soft, slow voice was Barbara's. She needed someone to talk to. Florance became her best friend. I did my best to be patient. Sometimes, I just had to say, "Barbara, I am busy. I have to go." Barbara collected key chains. Everywhere I traveled I bought a key chain for her. I had one from Italy in my pocket.

Twenty-one year after the settlement, I was visiting friends in Ft.; Lauderdale. I called Barbara and made a date to see her.

I knocked on the front door of a simple Florida ranch. I knocked again. Had Barbara forgotten about our meeting? It was entirely conceivable. After a few moments, the door crept open and Barbara, wearing large, red glasses, a pink sweatshirt and baggy blue athletic pants, greeted me. She led me into the house, where a medicinal smell lingered. Her movements were slow and labored— almost as though she was dragging a heavy object behind her. It explained her delay in reaching the door, and I could not help but notice her strained, slurred speech.

Ken, middle-aged, thin and very fit, joined us. He had a long nose, a drawn face, large round ears, very short, black hair and a thin goatee. He wore a gray polo shirt with a black collar and white khaki pants with a black belt.

"How are things going?" I asked.

Ken observed my furrowed brow and confided, "I've had 2 knee surgeries. They were tough, and my knees deteriorated afterwards. But that was nothing compared to a brain injury. Caring for a person who has a traumatic brain injury is a difficult and stressful task. Between doing laundry, managing finances, and handling medical bills and issues, it is at minimum a part time job."

Working as a bathroom renovator, Ken met hundreds, if not thousands, of people and families every year. Of the brain-injured people that he had met, many had stories similar to Barbara, of non-family members stepping up to take care of them. "They get excited when they find out that there are other people in similar situations. Sometimes it feels like you're alone out there," Ken exclaimed. "One thing Barbara is still adamant about is that she does not want to live in a 'facility'."

"What is it that has kept you caring for Barbara all these years?" I inquired.

"It is simply in my personality—I just cannot bear the thought of Barbara being alone and having no choice but to live in an institutional setting the thought of which she so loathes." Ken compared dealing with a brain-injured patient with raising a child. "One must constantly teach them and keep them away from things like the checkbook or the stove. However, in the case of traumatic brain injury this teaching must be repeated every few days or weeks for the rest of one's life. This can prove to be the most frustrating aspect of caring for a brain-injured person. Sometimes we get angry at each other. It is an unavoidable reality of a situation in which helplessness and irritation are familiar emotions. Afterwards, I always make it a point to apologize and explain to Barbara that it is not her I am frustrated with but the overall helplessness of her situation. I wish I could do more for her." Ken confessed he can get annoyed with Barbara's slow speech and her tendency to forget or misplace important items and documents, but he understood that she did the best she could, and that her injury limited her ability to process information quickly and remember things.

Barbara's expression turned morose. She looked at a picture of herself before the accident that was sitting on a table. Pointing at it, she said, "I haven't changed that much." Was Barbara still somewhat in denial? She was aware that she had lost some of her cognitive skills, but she did not realize the full extent to which she had. Her next comment revealed that she was just well enough to realize that she isn't well. "I have trouble understanding things that I knew perfectly before the accident. I sometimes forget memories that I had from before the accident, along with my short-term memory problems."

A brain that is injured takes longer and works harder to process information than a healthy one, and as a result Barbara, like many brain-injured people, had very little stamina and had to sleep a lot. Because her thoughts could be jumbled, she occasionally had trouble expressing herself in a way that was clear to other people.

I reflected on the brain-injured victims I had encountered and wanted to compliment Ken and tell him that he should leave his job and become a counselor to families of those who had unforgettable days. But I held my tongue because

Ken's present "job" was demanding enough.

Barbara spoke. "I find it difficult to stay in touch with old friends or make new ones. A lot of my friends are no longer my friends. One of the hardest things about coping with my brain injury has been dealing with the fact that I don't get many phone calls anymore."

"Most people do not understand what it means to be brain injured," Ken interjected. "They quickly become annoyed at her slow speech and inability to stay focused on a conversation, and often are unaware of or unwilling to recognize that she has memory problems. Barbara tries to compensate for her deficiencies and make friends by being extra nice to people. However, people that do not know her story often misconstrue this, especially if they are in a bad mood or in a hurry. Sometimes when Barbara is at a store, people get frustrated if she starts asking too many questions or holding up the check-out line."

Barbara agreed regretfully. "I wish I had more friends with whom I could go out to get a cup of coffee or go shopping. One of the things that provides me the greatest joy is going to the shopping center. It is a ten-minute walk and I make it a point to walk there, as I like to shop and my internist said that I needed to walk every day to keep up my strength. I also have access to a taxi service to drive me around. I made arrangements with them a day in advance and, because I am disabled, a round trip only cost four dollars. Without this service, I would be almost completely homebound. Yet even with this option, however, I still frequently stay at home. Still, the fact that I am within walking distance from the shopping center has been very important to me. I've made a few friends just by striking up conversations with people that I see walking around, and it gives me a break from my regular routine. It's something that I really cling to."

Like other brain-injury victims, Barbara relied on special "strategies" to help overcome the deficiencies that her injury had caused. She liked to wear bright, colorful clothing to cheer her up. To make up for her memory problems, she kept a logbook in which she wrote down things that she wanted to remember. She made sure to constantly check it to help remind her of commitments that she had and things she needed to do. She also kept a tape recorder in her pocket as another means of remembering important information. That way, she could record reminders to herself whenever they were needed so that she could play them back to refresh her memory as to what she had planned for the day. Using these and similar aids, she was able to raise her level of functioning. But there were still many things she was unable to do for herself.

We talked some more, reminiscing about the trial and other things. As I left Ken's house, I understood how difficult Barbara's situation was, but I thought to myself, "At the very least she is lucky to have someone like Ken who was willing to take her in and a place like the shopping center where she can spend time and make friends. At least Barbara has a few things in her life that she could cling to."

I was sitting at my desk several months later when my telephone rang. It was Barbara.

"I have a problem," she said.

"What's wrong?"

"Ken is moving into a new house. It is still in the same area, but much further away from the shopping center. I am very concerned about being alone at home all day. If he moves I will no longer have the opportunity to socialize and make friends. I feel like I am going down a stream with no paddle. The stream may be peaceful or turbulent but I have nothing to steer with, no way to slow down or change course. It seems like the only option left to me was just to hope for the best. I don't know what to do."

I did not know what to tell Barbara. Many brain injured people are cut off from others entirely, in their homes or in rehabilitation centers, and this serves both to isolate the brain injured person and also stymie growth of awareness of traumatic brain injury among the general public. For Barbara, like for millions of other brain-injured victims living a zigzag life, sometimes there was no right answer.

6. ALIVE. CLEAN AND SOBER

If only the jeep with a snowplow making its way out of the Chevy dealer's driveway had stopped? The driver looked to his right. All clear. A line of 1979 Suburbans on his left obstructed his view. Kate Brown's Mazda made its way cautiously on a two-lane highway with her son, Tom, and his friend, Andy, belted in the rear seats. The Jeep's engine revved. The snowplow crushed the Mazda driver's door.

Minutes later, a tall and big-shouldered EMT slid fourteen-year-old Andy onto a board, a flat sled that kept him off the ground. Ambulance lights carved wide red circles. A white plastic collar snapped around Andy's legs. An EMT belted his legs while another bandaged the gash on his forehead and then slashed open a sleeve on his coat. He wrapped a cuff around his arm. A snap snap locked the board into place. An EMT grabbed the ambulance door and pulled it closed.

A Medivac helicopter landed on a football field three miles away. A doctor wearing a lab coat over a pair of blue scrubs placed Andy's right arm on a cloth splint and fastened Velcro fasteners. An IV tube connected him to a plastic pack above her head. A heart monitor beeped.

"Code blue." "Doctor Levitt." Bells rang. Andy's brown eyes floated.

Andy's pelvis, spine and nine of his ribs were broken. His lung was punctured. The front right part of his brain pushed through a crack in his skull. Running a temperature of 106 degrees Fahrenheit, Andy hallucinated. He wouldn't remember the next six months.

Two weeks later, he was in a hospital bed attached to tubes and devices that measured his brain waves, heart rate, temperature, and blood pressure. His left arm was curled up close to his body. Ropes and pulleys lifted a casted right leg. A green wreath hung in Andy's antiseptic room and snow coated the sill outside a window.

Three weeks later, Doctor Ralph Weiss ushered me through a fluorescent-lit hallway with brown tiled walls and green linoleum floors in Jones Hall, a large brick building on the State university campus that had been converted into an infirmary and rehabilitation center. He opened a heavy blonde wood door. The room into which we entered was jam-packed with exercise equipment—parallel bars, stationary bicycles, floor mats, and weights, lots of weights. In the far right corner was a playpen, with mesh sides like the one Ellen and I once had in our living room when our children were infants. In the playpen, Andy's mother, Molly, lay next to Andy, brushing his hair and rubbing his back.

Right now, Andy can't talk. He can blink his eyes. He can hear and respond to simple commands, such as 'open your eyes,' or 'lift your head' but we don't know what he'll be able to do in the future. But we're putting him into some experimental treatments. The next three months are crucial," Doctor Weiss said. Molly looked up and forced a polite smile.

In his office, the doctor had a model of a skull on his desk. "This is the outer covering," he said, pointing. "It's bony and hard. Inside is the brain. It's soft and spongy. When the brain is traumatized, it swells up like a sponge absorbing water and the brain presses against the skull. Have you ever bruised your knee? If so, you know that it swells and hurts and you can't move it. Then the swelling goes down and you can move it. Something like that has happened to Andy. He was in a coma because the brain swelled and shut off his electrical system. The only things that were working were his sympathetic nerves, which control breathing. I opened his skull and reduced the pressure. Fortunately, Andy's brain is becoming less swollen, but he has already lost a lot of cells. They've died. It's called necrosis. We have no idea how many have died. There are millions and millions of them."

Doctor Weiss placed the skull on a credenza behind him and leaned forward. "Ten years ago, nine out of ten Andys didn't make it. Thanks to the helicopter and advancements in our emergency care, he's going to survive." He gestured toward the room with the playpen I'd just seen. "We're trying to find out if caring for a brain injured person as if he were an infant can teach undamaged brain cells to do the work the dead cells once did. Right now, his mother is living with Andy in that playpen."

Three months later, Dr. Weiss credited the infantile rehabilitation process for Andy's having relearned how to speak, eat, use the bathroom, brush his teeth and take a shower.

Andy navigated rehabilitation in a boat full of specialists—a neuropsychologist, who tested him to evaluate his thinking ability and behavior; physical therapists who taught him to walk again, get in and out of a wheelchair and helped him develop muscle tone and flexibility in his injured leg and arm; occupational therapists, who helped him relearn simple things like taking a bath; and speech therapists, who worked with him to lessen his flat speech.

During the past twenty years, I have encountered three people injured like Andy, who were given infantile rehabilitation. None of the people achieved success.

At fifteen and a half years old, after a year and a half in hospitals, both as an inpatient and outpatient, he still had short-term memory problems and could not concentrate when there were many people having conversations. Periodic grand mal seizures, which struck while he slept, left him with tremendous headaches.

Andy had just started 8th grade when the accident occurred. A shy kid, he was just becoming more social and making some friends. When he returned to school two years later, the school district offered to place him into 9th grade, so that he could stay on an almost normal track for graduation. Andy's parents decided that he would be better off repeating 8th grade. Placed in remedial classes, Andy, two years older than his classmates, felt out of place. His old friends avoided him. At 17, he was able to function somewhat independently and learned to drive.

The Chevy dealer did not own the snowplow. Since an independent contractor operated it, the Chevy dealer was not responsible so the snowplow's insurance was the only source of compensation. The snowplow's insurance company offered to settle with Andy for one million dollars, the limit of its policy. The snowplow driver didn't have anything but his Jeep, so Andy ended up with $750,000. In New Jersey, a lawyer earned 25% of the recovery for an injured client who was less than eighteen years old. With the aid of a financial planner, Andy invested $650,000 in secured annuities that would pay him a salary equivalent to one he would earn if he were working and which would grow with the rate of inflation. Every five years, Andy would receive lump sum payments until he was fifty. One hundred thousand dollars was placed in a money market account so Andy could purchase a car and have a feeling of independence. New Jersey's automobile insurance law covered his medical bills for the remainder of his life.

When he graduated from high school at 20, Andy went to a work-study program at a local rehabilitation institute. He enjoyed his first year, working with a mentor, learning how important it was to show up on time for work, how to push wheelchairs and how to teach wheelchair bound patients to use their chairs on uneven surfaces. But Andy often forgot where he was taking patients. He was the first brain-injured person to work there and the staff was not prepared to look after him. He was assigned paperwork, but didn't like it. He preferred physical work, like lifting people out of bed and pushing wheelchairs. At the end of the program, he was supposed to receive a job but did not, probably because the institute did not want to risk a lawsuit if Andy dropped or mishandled a patient because of his weak handgrip.

Despite advice from his parents and from me, he invested $80,000 in a restaurant. Six months later, he was unable to get along with his partner and he said, "Forget this," selling his share for a pittance. "You live and learn," he told his parents.

He volunteered at his local fire station, where he was on call 24 hours a day and had to be at the fire station ready to go within 5 minutes of an alarm. His task was to help the firefighters by rolling out the hoses and cleaning them after the fire had been put out. He enjoyed this job and the feeling of responsibility that came with it. Andy, lonely and insecure, wanted to be accepted. He went out for drinks with the guys at the firehouse and stopped for a six-pack on the way home. Andy began to drink, even though alcohol affected his brain injury.

A neurologist tried to cure him with sedatives to relieve anxiety but the medicine clashed with what he was taking for his seizures. So he went two hours a week to a psychologist who specialized in drug and alcohol addiction. When Andy repeatedly showed up for appointments late, under the weather, the psychologist gave up and notified the motor vehicle department that Andy was a danger to himself and to others on the road. His driving privileges revoked, Andy could not get to the firehouse.

Family members and friends convinced him to attend Alcoholics Anonymous meetings. His father took him to a church, three blocks from his home, to an "open" AA meeting where he was hooked up with a sponsor, who stopped by Andy's house and took him to meetings. It was a struggle, but AA and the friends he made there, along with the understanding, support, and encouragement of his family, helped him to adjust and finally to overcome his alcoholism.

Andy attended "closed" meetings where only people with personal drinking problems went. Andy liked the meetings, which began with socializing. He was celebrated as a newcomer, who was different from the other men and women in the group. Andy talked about his brain injury and, in so doing, learned that not many people knew what he was talking about.

He became extremely involved with AA and attended meetings two or three times a week. He regularly spoke out about his demon, his brain injury, during them. He was passionate about helping others overcome their demons and staying sober.

Andy was overcoming his drinking, but he still suffered grand mal seizures. Andy's parents were beside themselves. Several doctors prescribed ineffective medicine, but with no follow up to adjust the dosage. Despite taking up to nine pills a day, his seizures persisted.

They turned to me for advice. Insurance companies that were responsible for lifetime medical bills incurred by seriously injured people found that patients and doctors were taking advantage of a blank check so they contracted with agencies like the Visiting Nurses to monitor care and cut out unnecessary treatment both in institutional settings and home environments.

I contacted the insurance company that was paying Andy's medical bills and convinced them to hire an agency to monitor and coordinate Andy's care.

Kelly O'Malley, a woman in her forties, has a round face and blue eyes that emanates friendliness. A nurse with experience in intensive and rehabilitation care, she met with Andy, his parents and me in my office and then reviewed Andy's medical records. For three days over a period of two weeks, she got to know Andy intimately, following him as he went about his life. He had bouts of anger. Anti-depressants made him worse. Kelly found a doctor for him who diagnosed a chemical imbalance in the brain, and prescribed the right medication.

Kelly found out that Andy liked sports and had been a Boy Scout when the accident happened. Kelly got Andy involved in golf. Andy used his money to hire a golf pro and a guide with whom to do outdoorsman activities.

Now, free of seizures and much happier, Kelly introduced Andy to Community Options, an organization that helps people with disabilities. They had a job for him that involved interacting with brain-injured people in long-term care facilities and group homes, helping them get involved in the community by driving them to things they enjoyed, like bowling and pool. But Andy had no driver's license. Kelly steered Andy to a driving instruction course for the disabled. He got his license and the job.

Andy celebrated his thirtieth birthday. Andy had been working as a "community liaison." Kelly O'Malley and I pulled up to Andy's house, a white-and-brick-faced colonial with a maroon Chevy truck out front. Through wire-rimmed glasses that sat on a slightly upturned nose, I saw his light blue eyes. He limped into the living room and sat on a sofa next to his mother, who was battling throat cancer, gripping her hand. "Even now he cannot grasp things well with his right hand," said an electronic voice, activated by a button she pushed on a mechanical larynx.

Now seated at a table in a dining room filled with colonial furniture, heirlooms from Molly's family, who she said "came over on the Mayflower," my mind flashed back to the days after Andy's case was over when his father told me, "I worry about what will happen after I am gone." His mother had echoed, "I want to make sure that Andy is well taken care of." They had done all they could to provide for his future security.

Dinner over, Andy reminisced, "I still remember my time in the rehab. I remember what it was like to rely on others for tasks as simple as getting into and out of bed or moving from one room to another."

After Andy talked about what he remembered in rehabilitation, Kelly said, "Andy, you were lucky. I have seen my share of rehabilitation. The care is often poor, and it is not uncommon for callous aides to bump patients or handle them roughly when transferring them between beds and wheelchairs. The turnover rate is very high. Few people, who actually make an effort, work for long in this field. The most heavily injured patients—the ones that need the most care and attention—gain a reputation for being 'difficult' and 'a lot of work' and get switched around between different aides because no one wants to deal with them. It's a repeated process of victimization!"

"I used to say I was lucky, considering what I came back from, but I now say I am blessed. I can think, walk, talk and help others—there are many people out there who can't do that. When I'm pushing someone who is in a wheelchair, I remember being in one myself. I remember how scared I was, unsure if I would ever walk again." Andy said.

Kelly's face was a moon, smiling. "I work with patients who are paraplegics and quadriplegics. Andy, you are fortunate. I have seen so many people like that they fade away from society. A lot of them lose the will to live. They dream about playing football, running, riding a bike, but they realize that they cannot make their minds and bodies interact. They are already dead—they are just existing and waiting to die."

"I feel so bad for people who are paralyzed. I have pushed them. It's torture, really. They have it really bad. They're not like the ones that are badly brain injured. They know what's going on."

Andy's mother pushed the button on her throat. "I saw them after Andy's accident. People in wheelchairs, people on ventilators. They are bodies with heads speaking."

"Legally, they are able to refuse their treatment, but they can't unplug the ventilators and other machines themselves, and their caretakers cannot do it for them," Kelly said. "These people wake up in the morning wishing that they hadn't. They are like dead people living. What they were once is gone. They are new people. Different people. I try to get them to know their new 'me.'" Kelly looked at me. "You've been very quiet."

"I see what you see, but one of my jobs is to get money for people like the ones you and Andy are working with. I hope the money can bring the things the new 'me' needs in a new world. Sometimes, the money just pays for someone to brush your teeth, change your bed, or wipe the spit off your chin."

Andy's father cut in. "Nobody wants to think about an eighteen year old who broke his neck and will have to rely on a wheelchair for decades, especially when, with the nature of these kinds of accidents, your children or your spouse or even you yourself could be the next victim. What's sad is that this creates a vicious cycle. In every neighborhood, there are probably at least two or three people who are confined to a wheelchair or have a brain injury, but most people are not aware of them because most people in that condition are too ashamed and afraid to socialize and be seen publicly. Yet if the general public was better informed and had more opportunities to interact with people with these kinds of disabilities, they might understand them better and not shy away from them. This in turn would encourage more people with brain and spinal cord injuries to leave their homes and do things in public, making their lives more fulfilling and increasing their happiness."

"That's what I was so afraid of," Andy continued. "The loneliness. The isolation. Can you imagine that people as young as I was back then end up in nursing homes? Yet sometimes those are the only places that will take them."

Andy's mother pushed open a door from the kitchen, holding a chocolate cake with lighted candles. "Happy Birthday..."

Fascinated by how he devoted his time to helping others, I joined Andy as he spent a day with Bob, one of the people that he worked with through Community Options. We drove to the group home, where Bob, an African-American man in his mid-thirties, about six-feet two inches tall, had lived for fourteen years. He was eagerly awaiting our arrival. While Andy talked with Emilia, the staff person on duty, about his plans for the day, Bob told me about the games that he liked to play—pool, cards, Monopoly, and Uno, and showed me his room, with a framed, autographed Philadelphia Flyers jersey, Philadelphia Phillies and Eagles comforters and pillows, and a TV with built-in DVD and VHS players of which Bob was extremely proud. When he showed me his Trenton Thunder baseball team jersey, he excitedly explained that he and Andy planned a trip to a Thunder game in June.

Our first stop was the pizza shop that Andy had at once partly owned, where they were regulars. Bob shook hands with the employees and caught up, talking and joking, while Andy introduced me to his former business partner, Kevin. Kevin greeted and talked to me in between slicing deli meat. Understandably, most of his attention was focused on the meat cutter. Afterwards, Andy whispered to me, "That's why I got out of the business. I cut my hand too many times."

After lunch, we took a drive through Lambertville, the picturesque 150-year-old city with its quaint shops and the bridge connecting New Jersey and Pennsylvania across the Delaware River. Many people were out enjoying the first warm spring day. Diners sat on the patio of the Lambertville Station, a restored 1867 railway station now a famous eating establishment. People walked along the main street looking at galleries and antique stores. Cars and trucks with boats attached drove towards the riverfront. Bicyclers pedaled by in both directions. A woman tried to teach her longhaired golden retriever to swim in the river, but the dog seemed more interested in pawing through the wet mud.

We found a path by the river and walked along, passing well-decorated houses that stood invitingly by the bank of the Delaware. Shady trees, wind chimes, and the calm flow of the river added to the relaxing feel. Andy helped Bob, talking to him, holding his arm to make sure he did not get too close to the riverbank while Bob talked about country music. Willie Nelson was his favorite. He snapped a picture of Andy and me with his Polaroid camera.

All day, Andy listened, conversed, and entertained him. Bob was never anything less than an equal; never anything less than simply a friend.

This scene was all the more amazing when I considered how far Andy had come—organized, in charge, being able to look after not just himself but also another person—one who could not look after himself. Andy on that sunny day in April was a testament to how hard he had fought since awakening from a coma in 1980. He understood the challenges. However, Andy's superficial wellness masked the battles that he continued to fight. How could people unaware of brain injury believe that he was brain-injured when he walked and talked almost like normal? One could not notice the subtle yet essential tricks, strategies, and adjustments Andy employed that enabled him to interact with others. He carried a hand-held computer that beeped, reminding him of appointments. He had a telephone with a GPS that gave him directions from place to place. His shirt pocket was stuffed with yellow post-its, reminder notes he wrote out every day with his mother. His car keys and even his wallet were on a chain so that he would not forget them.

After I said goodbye, Andy told me, "My greatest foe in my recovery was my own denial of the situation and my refusal to accept the fact that I would have to live with this injury for the rest of my life. I was finally able to move on by focusing, not on the past which I could not change, but on the present, which is in my power. AA talks about living in the now. Letting go and staying in the now. It's a hard thing to do but it's what I must do."

Along with his job, Andy plays golf and is an avid outdoorsman, and he likes to go to the movies, especially with people he works with through Community Options. He used some of his settlement money to purchase the maroon Chevy truck parked in front of his house and driving enables him to stay active. Living at home, he helps his mother, who tires easily. Andy's parents worry about what will happen to him once they are gone.

Courageous as he is and fortunate to have the support of dedicated parents, and to have found Kelly O'Malley, it has taken years to come to terms with his limitations. But his involvement with Community Options and Alcoholics Anonymous turned into his life's passion. Inspiring and enhancing the lives of others who were unable to recover provides joy and meaning to his own life and perhaps even saved it. He gets lots of letters thanking him for volunteering.

7. THE LETTER

I get a lot of mail from prisons. The work of "jailhouse lawyers" arrives in stuffed brown envelopes containing letters and briefs typed on manual typewriters. Mary Christmas, an inmate at Trenton Psychiatric Hospital, deluged me with rambling descriptions of inter-planetary demons that made Jules Verne sound unimaginative. But often enough, a note like the hand-written one on my desk in November 1994, moves me to do something.

"I really died on April 12th, 1993," it began. "What remains," the writer went on to say, "is a shadow of what I was, a new entity woven of fear of what is and what remains to be encountered. My life is so dependent on my husband Barry that the thought of being separated from him is so terrifying as not to be allowed entry into my mind. My vulnerability without Barry would be horrendous. I cannot even think of such an event.

I am resigned to being a spectator of life's bounty—not a participant, not an achiever, not a winner, not an anything—just a waiter of day-by-day events in which I live on the periphery—in the shadows.

In the final analysis, the experience of my accident was not parallel to a specific trauma, which could beset an individual, such as an earthquake, rape or war. In each of these incidents just mentioned, a specific horror occurs from which one must extricate oneself and then try to repress the bad feeling and believe that the world is once more safe.

In the trauma I experience, emotional pain is an ongoing occurrence— starting with the first memory recall within the hospital walls and continuing day after day, week after week, month after month, and yes, even year after year. It isn't a one time bad thing; it is an everyday bad thing, because the brain is so slow in healing.

Day after day, I suffer the pain of loss of memory and visual recognition, and the struggle to relearn old information including subject matter content as well as teaching strategies. All this is overlaid with emotional suffering consisting of the fear of never getting better, the fear of disclosure, and the fear of economic, physical, and emotional vulnerability.

My doctor is not a brain injury doctor. He doesn't understand me. My family lawyer doesn't understand me either. Someone in my brain injury support group told me about you. You represented her after she was brain-injured. Will you help me?"

A few days later, I pulled up to a northern New Jersey home, a landscaped property with eclectic old farming equipment, fountains, and sculptures spread out around the house. A middle-aged woman with short red hair and a lively, animated face that radiated intelligence and a motherly kindness opened the door. She was Linda, the letter-writer, smartly dressed in a jacket with flowing, curvy designs in several shades of red and pink and a pair of black pants. A medium height, bespectacled man standing behind her was Barry.

In the kitchen, a former client sat at the table. Marsha's case, five years before, had been straightforward. A drunk driver had rear-ended her car and she, seeing double and vomiting, had been admitted to a hospital, where an MRI, a CAT scan and an EEG showed evidence of brain damage. Anyone who observed Marsha noticed her slurred speech and her inability to remember things that had just happened.

So far, Linda seemed alert and coherent.

"What happened?" I asked, taking a yellow pad out of my briefcase.

"I heard screeching brakes behind us. Barry had no time to react. Then there was the bang."

"How badly was the car damaged?"

"The bumper," Barry responded. "He pushed me forward. I was going for the gas pedal when he hit me. I had a big Buick and he had a little Valiant."

A car backfired on the street outside and two white poodles that had been lying quietly in the family room worked themselves into a frenzy, jumping at the window and barking like mad. In a calm yet firm tone, Linda said, "Don't bark, please. Settle down. You must stop immediately." The dogs calmed down and waddled toward her to get petted.

"I'm a teacher, you know," she said with a wry smile and a hint of a nervous chuckle. "I teach in an elementary school in a Gifted and Talented program and I love my job. I organize debates, discussions, mock trials, and economic programs for my students."

Barry reached for Linda's hand, leaned forward and his lips turned up. "She just won the state award for the best gifted and talented teacher."

Linda saw me jotting down notes on my legal pad and demanded: "You're writing that I'm alert and coherent, that I don't look brain-injured at all, aren't you?"

I replied that I wrote the former but not the latter.

She had no slurred speech, pained movement, or difficulty understanding what I said. She had not had any trouble performing a task like making coffee. I looked at Marsha, who had been comatose for a week and was left with short-term memory problems. What was wrong with Linda? Did she have memory loss problems, visual recognition problems? Did she struggle to relearn old information?

"Tell me about your memory problems," I said.

"I didn't remember any grammar and had to force myself to relearn how to speak." Her sentences and words were perfectly formed. Her letter had been well written. "If I hear something repeated several times in succession, I lose control and become angry."

"And visual problems?"

"I can't see colors. Some I can't see at all and others I see incorrectly. See that pink dishtowel. It's orange to me." Pink is orange, I thought. Was Linda a nut case like Mary Christmas? I erased the thought fast. I had represented people injured in low impact crashes that had a big impact on their life.

Linda squinted and her left cheek rose as if in pain. "You know what's most devastating? I cannot recognize faces. Can you imagine that? Every morning I wake up, and I cannot even recognize my own face in the mirror!"

"Just last night," Barry interjected. "We were at a dinner party. Linda was sitting next to a friend named Lonnie. Linda got up to go to the bathroom. Her friend Tim sat down where Lonnie had been sitting. When Linda got back, she continued her conversation with Lonnie!"

I tried to keep a poker face.

"Marsha, he's just like the others," Linda exclaimed.

"No he's not." Marsha rolled her eyes, embarrassed and took Linda's hand. She had supported Linda's return to teaching by calling her every morning while switching buses on her way to work. Marsha couldn't drive because sometimes she forgot where she was going, but the bus driver knew where to let her off and the other bus driver knew to pick her up. She knew firsthand what Linda was going through.

Linda had returned to her classroom on the pretense of cleaning things up, but her real purpose was to look through her materials and try to recall what and how she taught. She kept her injury secret, fearing that her students would play cruel jokes on her or the school administrators would let her go.

"How were you before the crash?"

Barry answered. "She was great at dealing with parents. She would win them over, persuade them that her plan about addressing their child's needs was right. That's why she got the award."

"If children came home complaining about me, their parents explained to them that I knew what I was doing," Linda said.

"Who at the school knew you very well?"

"The school principal."

"Any students?"

"A lot of them."

"Does one come to mind?"

"Billy Crawford."

"What has your doctor told you?"

"That she has a mild head injury," Barry said. "That really bothers her."

"I understand that," I said reassuringly.

Doctors, refer not to symptoms of brain injury, but to the initial trauma that caused it, used the term "mild head injury". To Linda, and unfortunately, to most people, the term "mild" implied that the injury was "not serious." My experience was that "mild head injury" prejudiced insurance companies and jurors against people like Linda.

Early in my career, I had represented a foot doctor injured in a crash similar to Linda's, leaving him with short-term memory problems and visual impairment. I presented evidence from a neurologist who explained that it was possible for brain injured people to experience no loss of consciousness at all and that the doctor's head injury led to alterations in his mental state. During the defense lawyer's cross-examination of the neurologist, he banged his head against a courtroom wall. The first time lightly, the second time harder, and the third time with a thud. He approached the doctor and asked, "Doctor, I don't have a brain injury, do I?"

"No," the neurologist replied.

"On Sundays you watch professional football players bang their heads against each other?"

"Yes."

"They don't have brain injuries, do they, Doctor?"

I lost the case because I believed the neurologist and was blind to the common belief that loss of consciousness and positive test results were required to prove a brain injury. I learned from that case that I needed not only testimony from the injured person and a doctor, but also that I had to demonstrate how my client's functioning had gone down after the accident. To do that, I needed testimony from people who knew Linda before and after.

Doctors had told Linda that she was a faker, just out for money. Barry showed me a report from the "independent medical group" to whom the driver's insurance company had sent her. They concluded, "Her symptoms and complaints are inconsistent with a diagnosis of traumatic brain injury and cannot be explained on the basis of any injury sustained in the April 12th, 1993 accident. Linda's complaints and difficulties are not genuine, brain-related deficits but instead are motivated by psychological factors such as marital distress, family issues, and other interpersonal factors. She is focused on litigation where she may recover secondary gain. Without the complicating influence of litigation, her symptoms should resolve and disappear."

I had read the same words written by defense experts in other cases. Insurance companies pay for well-qualified physicians with impeccable credentials, in the sunset of their careers, to become professional forensic witnesses. They attend seminars about how to prepare medical reports for court cases. The defense experts cited DSM IV-TR, the American Psychiatric Association desk reference dealing with one of the most challenging questions regarding mild traumatic brain injury—Can it be faked? Can litigants deliberately or even unintentionally intensify the severity of their symptoms? Defense experts often used headaches, depression, and other subjective complaints and the lack of "objective physical findings" as proof that patients presenting as having suffered traumatic brain injury were in fact suffering from an injury which they believe occurred but which had not.

After Danish and coffee, Linda signed releases that permitted me to get her hospital and doctors' records. Armed with them, I began to seek ammunition to use to win Linda's battle. I discovered that she had not lost consciousness. There was no evidence that she had struck her head. No MRIs, CAT scans, or EEGs had been taken. Her school and work records indicated that she had always been bright, ambitious, and motivated until shortly after April 12th, 1993.

Joseph Keefe, the principal, had a Marine buzz cut and a red beard that framed blue eyes and a broad nose. He recalled the day approximately three weeks after Linda's accident that she shuffled into his office and said in a tone that echoed frustration, "I have to tell you something. I know who you are because there's a sign on your door. I don't recognize your face. After I got out of the hospital, I couldn't believe it. I didn't recognize Barry. Then I couldn't recognize other people and had to ask them who they were. I couldn't believe it—I didn't even recognize myself in the mirror! And then, I got colors all mixed up. My doctor has told me it'll go away, but it hasn't. I need your help until this nightmare ends."

"I'm a victim of glaucoma," Keefe said. "So I understand something about disability. I suggested she use nametags in class and promised her that I wouldn't tell any of her fellow teachers until she told me it was okay to say something. Linda stayed out of the teacher's room and confined herself to her classroom for a few weeks."

He described how Linda practiced with grammar books used by the sixth graders. "She wrote essays. They became a game and were read by her fellow teachers. She overcame her writing problems but she still needs nametags. Have you seen her clothes? They are color labeled. Linda's always been a tough and stick-to-it person. That's why she's so good at what she does."

Billy Crawford's parents, Kevin and Anne, knew Linda before and after her accident. Anne said that Linda stayed in touch with her students' parents. She would discuss how Billy was doing in her class and what they were studying. Since the accident, Kevin said, "She hasn't been herself. When she passes me on the street, she ignores me. Once I waved at her to get her attention. It didn't seem like she recognized me until after I introduced myself as the father of one of her pupils and told her my name."

Dr. Goldstein, Linda's doctor, was a general practitioner who had cared for her for years, treating her for colds, a urinary infection and a bad case of poison ivy. Her annual physicals were unremarkable. His records contained one episode of anxiety, precipitated by Barry's losing his job as a patternmaker at a company at which he had worked for a number of years. Dr. Goldstein thought Linda's visual complaints and memory complaints would fade away as her writing and grammar problems had faded away. Although he had no neurological training and was not qualified to give a medical opinion about brain injury, he could testify to what Linda was like before and after the accident. He had not referred Linda to a brain injury specialist because she had recovered from some of the things that she complained about and "was a determined lady. She even joined a brain injury support group on her own."

I was satisfied that I had enough information to establish a pre-accident baseline that would demonstrate how the accident altered Linda's functioning.

Dr. Jeffrey Brown, a neuropsychiatrist and lawyer, is a recognized expert on both the clinical and legal aspects of traumatic brain injury. A doorman at a posh Park Avenue apartment house buzzed Dr. Brown's office.

I was ushered into an office where four soft leather armchairs were arranged in a square around a light yellow table. A muscular man with a chiseled chin and close-cropped, receding hair entered the room. He wore a white shirt, a red tie, dark blue pants, and maroon shoes. I had sent Linda's letter, her hospital records, Dr. Goldstein's notes, and the defense expert report to him after I made the appointment.

He said he thought Linda had suffered a brain injury.

Dr. Brown reached toward a table and cradled a model of a skull. He unhinged the top part and ran his fingers along the interior edge of the skull. "You see how rough, bony, and ridgy this is? Especially near your forehead and ears? That's where your frontal and temporal lobes are." He looked up at me. "Right now your brain is floating in fluid – cerebrospinal fluid. But let's say somebody came behind you and pushed your chair real hard. An abrupt movement can cause the brain to strike the bony ridges of the skull. When the head goes back and forward quickly, the brain can be bruised and bleed and sometimes the axons are stretched and torn. I think that's what happened to Linda. These bruises can cause short-term memory loss, language problems, and visual perception problems like the ones Linda has."

"So how can I prove what you suspect is true? There's no MRI, there's no CAT scan, and there's no EEG."

"The type of injury Linda has is so microscopic it's difficult to detect even with advanced diagnostic tools."

"The insurance doctor says Linda is a faker."

Dr. Brown grinned. "Because he said that, that's how you can win the case. Linda can come here and I can give her neuropsychological tests that will locate where her brain has been damaged."

I raised my eyebrows and asked, "What about the faking?"

"The woman who wrote that letter isn't faking."

A lack of understanding of the nature of brain injuries, in the courts and from the public, was something we both had witnessed. Someone who has had a stroke or a broken bone is easier to represent because people can see the injury. A person with a brain injury, especially a relatively mild one like Linda's, is more difficult because she looks normal on the surface.

"Most people tend to get their information about brain injury from high-profile athletes and celebrities whom they watch on television that have suffered such injuries," Brown responded. "People might see an athlete who will quickly come back to the playing field after one concussion and won't retire until he has suffered seven or eight of them, not realizing that even one causes severe neurological damage and cognitive deficiencies and that such athletes are risking their health in coming back to play."

We agreed that brain injury has become stigmatized due to this misguided perception that traumatic brain injury can be less severe than some experts claim. "In the public perception, the term 'closed head injury' has become like the new 'TMJ,'" I bemoaned, referring to temporomandibular joint disorder – inflammation of the joint that connects the lower jaw to the skull – that was an infamously common misdiagnosis for victims of rear-end collisions in the 1980s. "Nevertheless," I added, "I do not consider the legal system to be biased against brain injured people per se, but proving a traumatic brain injury in court can be challenging when the defense can present experts to contest claims and play to people's perceptions while the victim may not, on the surface, look hurt."

Over the course of two months, Linda met with Dr. Brown three times for evaluation and testing. He used the Wechsler Memory Scale-III test, in which Linda was required to recall sentences and lists of words that had been read aloud to her both immediately and after a 30 minute delay. He tested her ability to recall visual detail by briefly presenting pictures to her and then asking her to recall the details. He administered the Minnesota Multi-phasic Personality Inventory (MMPI), which showed that Linda was not faking her injury. The test when used by a trained professional assists in identifying personality structure and psychopathology. Dr. Brown also used the MMPI-2F test, a recent development that used rigorous statistical methods to detect faking.

His report concluded that "the neurobehavioral deficit which has been objectively documented and elucidated above is directly attributable to the accident in question" and that "her current level of cognitive-neurological functioning reflects significant compromise relative to her premorbid levels." Plus, he hastened to add:

"The possibility that the patient is making a conscious or unconscious attempt to present in a highly unfavorable light has successfully been ruled out.

It should be noted that a significant period of time has elapsed since the patient's cerebral insult. Therefore, I can state within a reasonable degree of medical probability that the difficulties with which this patient presents may point to residual impairment that is long-term, enduring, and permanent."

The insurance company for the driver that hit Linda and Barry had her reexamined. Their neuropsychiatrist concluded that Linda was not faking, but he interpreted his data to mean that Linda's problems were the result of obsessive-compulsive behavior that caused her to exaggerate. According to him, this behavior was psychosomatic.

The battle lines were drawn. Not only was Linda's believability in question, but also Dr. Brown's credibility was at stake.

Jimmy Woodruff, the attorney who had defeated the foot doctor, was on Linda's case.

"A brain injury? Are you kidding me? You're banging your head against a wall," he smirked. "This woman was conscious at the scene, her tests all came back normal, and she was able to go back to work. I'm going to have a field day with this if it even gets to trial."

I described Linda's problems since the accident, explaining that experts would back up her claims.

His voice had an air of confidence: "Who's the jury gonna believe? They'll be wary of the 'experts' and all I have to do is show them the tests. On the stand, she'll look and sound so good, a jury'll never buy what she's saying. It'll be a piece of cake to convince them she's just out for money. You can forget about my client making an offer."

The defense submitted interrogatories, written questions that Linda and Barry had to answer under oath. When I met with them to write out properly formulated responses, Linda became agitated about reliving the nightmare again and then morose. "I guess it is too much to hope to find justice through the legal system," she said.

"Don't say that. The battle is far from over."

Two months later, I prepared Linda for her deposition, warning her that Woodruff's questions would use any imprecise words or phrases of hers to try to corner her. He would expose any inconsistencies in her story to imply to the jury that if they could not trust her to recount details of her life before and after the accident, how could they believe her claims of suffering a brain injury?

Linda sat very stiffly, her eyes staring out into space as though lost in her own thoughts.

"The defense lawyer is going to play up my normal appearance and play up the fact that I went to work? He's gonna ask the jurors to question how injured I really am?"

"That's right."

"Will they offer anything to settle?" Barry asked.

"I don't think so. They have a better chance trying their luck outright with a jury. They've made no offer."

Linda frowned. "What was I supposed to do? If I hadn't gone back to work, they would claim I was out for money. I desperately wanted to go back to my job and reestablish normalcy in my life. I didn't want someone else's mistake to take that away from me."

I knew losing hope was the worst thing that could happen to a victim of brain injury.

When Jimmy Woodruff entered and introduced himself, Linda stood up and shook his hand. She asked me for a sheet of paper, folded it in half and printed with a felt tip pen she took from her pocketbook: "Mr. Woodruff."

"What's this?" he asked.

"A nameplate," she replied.

During an hour and a half of questions, Linda responded, addressing Woodruff as "Sir" and "Mr. Woodruff." She "taught" Jimmy Woodruff about her brain injury.

Nine months later, the day of the trial arrived. Judge Margaret Keller was a no-nonsense judge, getting right down to business in her chambers.

"What does the plaintiff assert?"

I said the car accident left her with a brain injury that affects her ability to perform her job and strains her marriage and personal relationships. We were asking for compensation.

Woodruff's usual demeanor, which had earned him the nickname of "The Bulldog" for tenaciously going after his opponents and refusing to let go, was replaced by a look that suggested he was open to compromise. "Your Honor," he said, "I believe her claims of injury are justified, but I don't think they're worth half a million dollars. I have been authorized to make an offer of one hundred thousand dollars. It's a generous offer."

Judge Keller suggested I should inform my client that this is the most equitable settlement that she could expect to receive because very few people with closed head injuries win their cases. Linda and Barry were standing outside

Judge Keller's courtroom. They followed me into an empty office, where I explained the offer.

For the first time in a long time, a look of hope crept into Linda's expression. I knew that she would take the deal. "What is he offering?"

"One hundred thousand dollars."

"How much will Linda receive?" Barry asked.

In my mind, I calculated my one-third fee and added the approximately fifteen thousand dollars in costs I had expended for medical examinations and experts' reports.

"A little over fifty thousand," I replied.

"That's not a lot of money," Linda said. "If it means that I won't have to relive the accident again, maybe it is enough?"

Barry looked at me. "Give me an honest answer. Do you think we can win?"

"We have a strong case, but you know as well as I do that the jurors could think that if they can't see it or hear it, it must not be there." I explained that most people think that a mild traumatic brain injury is not disabling, not serious or permanent, and that its effects must be immediate, otherwise it doesn't exist. Worse yet, most people believed you had to hit your head and be unconscious to get a brain injury.

Barry exhaled audibly and his mouth became a taut line. To Linda, he said, "Honey, this offer is good, but what you've wanted all along is vindication. I know it will be hard to talk about the accident yet again, but to hear a jury tell you that you were wronged? That you are not faking? That you deserve justice? I think that would be worth more than any settlement."

"Can I talk to Barry alone?" Linda asked.

I walked to the far end of the courtroom hallway. At the water fountain, I gulped some water. My throat was dry.

Barry signaled me with his hand. They met me halfway.

"Barry is right," Linda said. " We're going to take our chances with a trial."

The trial began that afternoon with voir dire, the process of selecting jurors. One by one, the potential jurors introduced themselves and answered questions posed by Judge Keller. By the end of the day, Jimmy Woodruff and I were both satisfied with the makeup of the jury. Judge Keller adjourned for the day.

The trial commenced at 9:30 the next morning. I called witnesses to the stand, beginning with Linda and continuing on to Barry, Joseph Keefe, the Crawfords and Dr. Goldstein. After each witness left the stand, I glanced at the jury box, but their expressionless faces gave me no hint as to what they were thinking.

I called my last witness, Doctor Jeffrey Brown, who explained to the jury that not all mild head injury victims ended up okay. About 15% ended up with a deficit that affected their thinking and their ability to see things accurately. With the model of the skull, he explained how Linda's brain was bruised without being struck and her being unconscious. With his test results, he justified his conclusion that Linda had a permanent injury that affected her visual perception and an injury that resulted in a language deficiency, which Linda, through her tenacity, was able to compensate for.

The jury listened attentively when he said that most of the recovery in brain injuries occurred within six months after the trauma. Linda's language deficiencies were overcome within that time. But now, three years later, Linda still had the visual recognition problems and the chances of her recovering from them were slim. He explained to the jury that Linda was lucky to have Dr. Goldstein, who knew her before and after her accident, because so many people with injuries like Linda's face a problem because the injury isn't readily visible.

When the defense doctor was midway through his testimony, I noticed a few jurors lean backward and fold their arms. To me, that meant that the jurors did not believe the defense doctor and had turned him off.

Jimmy Woodruff summed up, arguing that while his client was negligent and caused the accident, Linda did not suffer the injuries she claimed from the impact that left only minor damage to Barry's bumper. Two jurors subtlely shook their heads from side to side.

I said that it was my job to bring Linda's story to them through witnesses who knew her before and after the collision and that if they believed the witnesses whose testimony was supported by a reputable neuropsychiatrist, it was their job to permit Linda to leave the courthouse fairly compensated for an injury she had no role in causing.

The jury retired. An hour and a half later, the jury had a question. They wanted a definition of 'pain and suffering.'

"Oh well," I said to Woodruff. "One of us is going to leave the courthouse today unhappy."

The jurors were in the jury box when we returned to the courtroom and Judge Keller was on the bench. She gave them the answer:

"If you find for Linda, she is entitled to recover fair and reasonable money damages for the full extent of … any permanent and any temporary injury resulting in disability to or impairment of her faculties, health, or ability to participate in activities as a direct result of the defendant's negligence or wrongdoing. Disability or impairment means worsening, weakening, or loss of faculties, health, or ability to participate in activities. It includes the inability to pursue one's normal pleasure and enjoyment. You must determine how the injury has deprived Linda of her customary activities as a whole person. This measure of damage is what a reasonable person would consider to be adequate and just … to compensate Linda for her injury and her disability, impairment, and the loss of enjoyment of life."

Forty-five minutes later, the jury announced its verdict: $575,000.

Jimmy Woodruff, a tough but fair advocate, shook my hand.

"How come you didn't bang your head against a wall like you did in the foot doctor's case?" I asked.

"I didn't think it would work. Linda's a woman and I was afraid that it would backfire." Woodruff smiled. "A lawyer gives three summations. The one that he has prepared to give, the one he delivers, and the one he thinks he should have delivered after the case is over. Maybe I should have banged my head against the wall," Woodruff added, chuckling.

Linda and Barry received enough money, which if invested prudently, would provide for a nice retirement. They were happy to finally put the case behind them and as usual, as other clients and other cases began to occupy my attention, they slowly faded from my mind.

Fifteen years later, they had moved to a gated retirement community. Their new living room was drenched with sun from the large windows. Sitting on a plush, brown sofa, I stared at a copy of Fredric Remington's Bronco Buster standing on a glass table and noticed a book with John Lennon and Yoko Ono on the cover.

Linda sat quietly for several long moments. "I am very grateful for what you did for me, but sitting here now and talking to you, it brings up so many bad memories. Over the years I've thought of calling you, or responding to the birthday cards you've sent, but these all serve as reminders of the interrogatories, the depositions, the trial – being forced to relive the accident again and again."

"I wish I could go back and change what happened. I remember when you gave us our money. It was in a brick building right across the road from here. If not for that, we would not be in this room right now. That's the way I try to look at my injury now, from a cost-benefit standpoint. The benefit has been that we haven't needed to manage our retirement. The verdict took some of the pressure off us financially and it gave me peace of mind. But I'd much rather not suffer from the problems I still have."

Linda had lost a lot of friends in the years after the accident and she was upset at their failure to visit and comfort her immediately after it happened. "A psychiatrist advised me to confront them directly. Looking back I understand this as an example of my over reliance on others' opinions. It's what I now try to avoid. I lost several friends doing what the psychiatrist suggested. At the same time, my inability to recognize faces made making new friends nearly impossible. I can meet someone at a party one evening and then pass them on the street the very next day and completely ignore them. Without knowing my story, they assume that I'm being unfriendly and get offended."

"On the surface Linda looks fine," Barry said. "So people don't understand the deficits she has."

"In a way, though, I prefer it like that," Linda admitted, looking at the ceiling. "I don't want people I meet to think of me as a head case. I don't want special treatment— just to be able to go on with my life and not let my injury alter it. That's why it was so important to return to teaching."

"Linda's desire for normalcy, her ability to survive and overcome her injuries, is remarkable," Barry said, beaming with pride.

"I was once told, 'don't ask what your disabilities are, ask what your abilities are,'" Linda said. "I have tried to think of that in times of stress, when I was angry or depressed about not being able to do something as quickly or as well as I used to."

She and Barry had been worried about not winning because "I thought that jurors, being ordinary people, would be liable to judge more on how a person appeared than on any other evidence. Their instinct would tell them that a person that appeared outwardly normal was uninjured, and I was really afraid I'd end up with no compensation. It is so unfair!" Linda was animated. "Just because I could walk and I didn't slur my words didn't mean that I didn't have an injury or that I was looking for a handout."

"The whole system ought to be changed. I would have much rather gone to a specialized brain injury court in which an experienced judge with an understanding of what it means to be brain-injured would hear and decide the case. Sure, I'm wary of a system that would be too easy to abuse, but I believe that experts, not a jury, are needed to decide cases like mine. Dr. Goldstein – he's a good family doctor but he didn't know enough about brain injury to help. He thought that because some of my problems were getting better, there was no need to refer me to a specialist. The lawyer before you thought I had no case."

Linda was angry and Barry explained why. "It is hard to put her faith in anyone. Brain-injured people go through a second childhood. They have no background of experiences to know when someone is putting their own interests ahead of theirs. That's why it is so important to find people who understood brain injury. When people don't understand them or take advantage of them, they learn not to trust anyone."

When I handed Linda the blank release giving me permission to use her story in my book, she read it carefully and when she ran across a statement she did not like, she crossed it out without hesitation and rephrased it. Her disgust with legal documents and terminology was evident as she wrote out a new sentence explicitly denying me permission to use her real name and likeness. Any person observing this would not believe that she had a disability.

As I walked towards the door, Linda touched my arm. "I have something for you that might be good in your book." She handed me a single sheet of paper. It was her letter —the one that my secretary had told me to make sure I took a look at all those years before.

Linda's case was the most beguiling I had ever handled. That was until I represented Josh.

8. THE LEGACY

Josh Bryant, a handsome, tall young man with the sculpted figure of a weightlifter, was the town character, strutting around the tight-knit community of Medford, New Jersey or wheeling around in his orange Pontiac GTO. He learned to operate computers at the local community college, worked nights and weekends at Radio Shack, fiddling with gadgets in his spare time. After graduation, he got a job with an aerospace company, where he rose from assembly line worker to floor manager within a year.

Working for a corporation didn't mesh with Josh's free spirit, so he opened his own photography business. His photos of covered bridges, barns and muscle cars won awards and appeared in Time, Newsweek and the New York Times. Within two years, he was able to buy his own house, a three-room log cabin bungalow, where he built shelves for the 5000 vintage beer cans that he had been collecting since he was thirteen and the miniature model cars he bought at flea markets. His photographs hung on what walls were left. A room was devoted to pinball machines and Nintendo that Josh played hours on end. The panes on the front door sported Philadelphia Eagles decals.

Josh met Lorraine at a muscle car show where she was a cashier. After two months of courting, Lorraine moved in and six months later became his fiancee. Josh was twenty-eight years old. Life was good. One thing bothered him. Pasta, fast foods, and too many beers and pretzels with his friends, all Philadelphia Eagles fanatics, had taken their toll. He was overweight and flabby. When a diet center opened in town, Josh signed up.

On his way to the DIET CENTER, Josh's GTO veered off the two-lane macadam road and bounced 768 feet across the Blue Grass Sod Farm before it struck a tree and burst into flames.

When Josh's brother and girlfriend came to my office a month later, they were "looking to sue GM." I had just won a case against General Motors for a couple who had been driving home from an Eagles game when a car being chased by one of Philadelphia's finest swerved to avoid a trolley car and hit their Chevy Nova head on. An anchor bolt securing the wife's passenger seat belt fractured, sending her through the windshield.

Thanks to Ralph Nader, automobile manufacturers have to comply with certain safety regulations. Nader's book, <u>Unsafe at Any Speed</u>, uncovered the Chevrolet Corvair's unsafe suspension system and exposed rear gas tank in 1965. The Federal National Traffic and Motor Vehicle Safety Act of 1966 set standards for seat belts and their components. Regulation FMVSS #209 required seat belts and anchors to withstand a force of 2500 pounds.

I hired John McDougal, an engineer who specialized in accident reconstruction. He ran four Chevy Novas with dummies the wife's size and weight through crash tests at a laboratory in Annapolis, Maryland. The forces from the collision of the two cars, he proved, should not have caused the Nova's anchor bolt to fail. Even though the law in accident cases only requires proof that a defective product caused an injury by a preponderance of the evidence, that is, by making the scale of justice tip ever so slightly, by a feather, in his or her favor, I had lost cases because jurors wanted to know if passengers like the wife would have been injured even if the seat belt had not failed.

To make sure that a jury could see that she would not have hit the dashboard, let alone the windshield, the same model Chevy Nova was cut in half and fitted with wheels like the ones on rolling suitcases and wheeled into the Philadelphia courtroom. Marie, the injured passenger, sat in the front seat, fastened her seat belt and yanked it. She leaned forward, demonstrating that her head could not have reached the dashboard. A few hours later, G.M.'s lawyer offered to settle.

Her husband, Ziggy, who had been driving the car, was an engineer who then became obsessed with lawsuits against automobile manufacturers. "When Marie was pregnant," he said, "all I saw were pregnant women. Now, all I see are defective cars." Ziggy was a big Eagles fan and his seats at VETERAN'S STADIUM were two rows behind Josh Bryant and his brother, Tim. When he noticed that the brothers had missed two games, he called. Tim told him about Josh's accident and that, burned over 70 percent of his body, Josh was clinging to life in the Crozer Chester Burn Center. "Dammit, a Ford Pinto case," Ziggy said.

In May 1972, Lily Gray was traveling with thirteen year-old Richard Grimshaw in a 1972 Ford Pinto when their car was struck by another car traveling approximately thirty miles per hour. The impact ignited a fire, which killed Lily Gray and left Richard with devastating injuries. A jury awarded the Gray family $560,000, Grimshaw $2.5 million for compensatory damages and punitive damages of $125 million, later reduced to $3.5 million.

The Pinto's fuel tank was placed behind the rear axle instead of above it, to create more trunk space. The gas tank and axle were only nine inches apart. There were also bolts holding the axle, positioned in a manner that threatened the gas tank, and the fuel filler's pipe design made it likely that it would disconnect from the tank in an accident, causing gas spillage and fire. Since a product adjustment would cost $11 dollars per car or $137 million for the 11 million cars and 1.5 million trucks on the road, Ford decided to take the risk of being sued. The result was 180 deaths, 180 burn injuries, and 2100 burned vehicles in one year. At $200,000 per death, $67,000 per injury, and $700 per vehicle, Ford figured it would have to pay out $49.5 million dollars in the worst case, saving almost $100 million dollars.

Ziggy told Josh's brother to call me and, "He'll sue G.M. for you."

I met Tim and Lorraine in the lobby of the Crozer Chester Burn Clinic. On Josh's floor, the door bore a decal—INFECTION CONTROLLED AREA RING FOR ASSISTANCE. A nurse ushered us into a room where we had to wash our hands, put on white gloves and wear cover gowns and masks.

Tim and Lorraine waited outside while Dr. Haith and I went in. I had dropped out of pre-med in college because the dogfish I dissected looked like chopped herring and the embryo I extracted ended up scrambled. The sight of blood made me queasy. As a child, I had seen a neighbor being pulled out of a window filled with flames and carried down a ladder and placed in an ambulance, where he would breathe his last breath. My greatest fear is being burned.

What I could see of Josh's body was burnt to a crisp. His hands had been burned off. Peeking out of a sheet that went from his chest to his ankles were feet bandaged like a mummy.

"Does he feel any pain?" I asked.

He shook his head from side to side. "He's totally sedated."

"What are his chances?"

"Slim to none. I've never seen anyone burned over 70% of his body survive."

In the lobby, Tim and Lorraine waited on a bench.

"What do you think?" Lorraine asked.

Tim said, "If we have a case against G.M, what are our chances?"

I explained that under New Jersey law an injured person who did not experience conscious pain and suffering would not be awarded damages. Only if he survived and experienced pain would he would be entitled to money. If Josh died, only survivors who were dependent on him would be able to collect money, but he and Lorraine were not married. Even if a case were proven against GM, it would not warrant significant monetary damages. Despite being flabbergasted, they agreed that I would conduct a preliminary investigation and, if by some miracle, Josh hung on, we would work together.

John McDougal and I visited the junkyard where the Pontiac GTO was stored, ready for the automobile graveyard. McDougal had also worked on Chevy Corvair and Ford Pinto cases and was consulting with a California lawyer who was contemplating suing Chrysler in a case that involved a Plymouth that had been hit head on and caught fire.

McDougal examined the front of the GTO and remarked, "He wasn't going that fast. Probably about 30." That made sense. The speed limit on the rural road was 40 M.P.H. and traveling 700 feet across a grassy field would slow up the vehicle unless Josh's foot was pressing on the accelerator. If he had done that, it would be more like suicide than an accident.

The car's left side door had been removed and rested against a nearby fence. McDougal was on his knees, fingering the seat belt bracket. "It failed," he exclaimed, his eyes big as eight balls. "You may have a case. If the driver hit the tree and the seat belt failed, he would have hit the dashboard and got knocked out. If he hadn't hit the dashboard and got knocked out, he could have had time to get out of the car."

"You're kidding?"

"No, I'm not. Look at the floor panel over there." He pointed to the crushed floor panel in front of the passenger seat. McDougal measured the crush of the car, photographed it outside and inside, and asked me to document, using his camera, his removal of the fractured seat belt bracket.

General Motors was in my sights again.

Winning against GM was no easy task. I had spent over $80,000 representing Marie. Contingent fees, where the lawyer collects one-third of a recovery, are supposed to enable a lawyer to represent injured people whose rights have been infringed upon and cannot afford what it takes to fight for their rights. Marie would help Josh, if he hung in long enough to make the fight worthwhile.

The Medford Police report described the Pontiac GTO "against a large pine tree, the front engine compartment on fire. And a driver pinned behind the wheel. A witness saw the car going 40 M.P.H. when it swerved suddenly to the left and proceeded across the Blue Grass Sod Farm and hit the tree. He noted that the driver made no attempt to stop before the collision."

A bell sounded. What if the tie-rod that keeps the wheels in line broke? I had won a case in which that had happened on a Jeep. I immediately got on the telephone to McDougal.

"I don't think that's what happened," he said. The tire tracks from the road to the tree were straight as an arrow. "I'll get one of the mechanics to take a look underneath."

About an hour later, McDougal called back. "The tie-rods are all connected. The impact is all on the right side. If Josh were trying to kill himself, he would have steered so the tree was directly in front of him. Something doesn't add up here."

McDougal's preliminary report concluded "the driver's head injuries were caused by the failure of the seat belt anchor allowing him to impact the windshield frame and windshield. The burns were increased in severity by his inability to get out of the vehicle." He was really puzzled about why Josh would swerve sharply to the left while he was on the road. Perhaps the witness could answer that question.

Back at Crozer Chester with Tim and the white gloves, gown and mask, Josh's doctors had initially given him a 2% chance of surviving and tried to convince his family that he wasn't going to make it. They were going to let him go, but Tim and Lorraine insisted they try everything. Now, he was, to everyone's surprise, surviving. "He shouldn't be," a nurse said, adding, "His quality of life will be a world of hell if he makes it. The nurse called Josh "Ali." Josh tried to force his lips into a smile. He opened his eyes wide. "You're a fighter," she said, lifting the sheet. He had been so badly burned that the sweat glands on the parts of his body that had been affected were destroyed. Only his head could still sweat, so if the temperature got too high, his head would overflow with sweat and he couldn't withstand temperatures above 72 degrees.

Mark Green, the witness, was short, stocky, and bald, with a dark reddish beard, long, light eyebrows, and a bulging forehead. "I couldn't believe my eyes. We were moseying along. It was a beautiful fall morning. All of a sudden the driver in front of me slumped forward onto the steering wheel. The car went left and across the field at an angle. I watched it. It was like slow motion. The head never rose. I kept waiting to see shoulders rise. Something. It was like he passed out," he said.

McDougal said that Mark Green's account destroyed his theory. If Josh was unconscious before the collision, he would not have awakened on impact and the fault was clearly not GM's. McDougal repeated what he had told me before I hired him. "If I find reason to sue the car manufacturer, I will say so. But if a defective product was not the cause of injuries, I will tell you that. Leading an injured person down a primrose path is wrong. There is no reason to be a victim twice. I won't be a hired gun, who just says what some lawyer wants me to say, hoping that they can extract money from someone."

I felt the same way. I'd deliver the bad news as soon as I could get Tim and Lorraine together.

Tim had been spending almost every waking hour at Josh's bedside, making small talk with his brother, who was conscious but motionless. Doctors had told him that people burned as badly as Josh had hope and every breath of life that they could hear kept them connected to life. Tim nodded as I told him what John McDougal had found and what he had concluded. Lorraine's head dropped as she wiped her eyes and then tears cascaded down her cheeks.

I cannot stand to see a woman cry. I cry once a year during the trophy presentation to the woman who wins the Wimbledon tennis championship. Mine are tears of joy. Lorraine's were not. I buzzed a legal assistant and Kathy, a paralegal, tiptoed into my office with a box of Kleenex and pulled up a chair next to Lorraine.

Sipping a glass of water, she blurted, "It's my entire fault. He passed out in the bathroom. I brought him to. I should have driven him, but he insisted he was alright."

Lorraine turned to Tim. "You know Josh. When Josh makes up his mind about something, you don't cross him."

Tim nodded.

"We had a fight before he stomped out to the car." Lorraine wiped more tears away. "Ever since he went on that diet he wasn't right. He was groggy and forgetful. He lost so much weight so fast. He was cranky and edgy. Not himself. But he was hell bent to lose that weight. If only I had driven him!"

I assured her that what befell Josh was not her fault, not anyone's fault.

Kathy, the paralegal, had fought being overweight for as long as I knew her. She had been on every diet imaginable. Nutri-Systems. Jenny Craig. Weight Watchers. She ushered Lorraine out of the office to freshen up.

"That was some act, wasn't it?" Tim said the second the door closed. "She told me last night that she was moving into an apartment in North Jersey with her sister. She's breaking the engagement. What a bitch. If Josh makes it, this will kill him."

Kathy came back in after they left to tell me that some things Lorraine said had raised a red flag in her mind and she was going to go to that Diet Center. Kathy was that kind of legal assistant. She thought out of the box and liked to play detective. And she did, on the pretense that she wanted to join the program and lose weight. She filled out a "Personal Review" with a symbol DIET CENTER on it, a form called "Present Eating Habits," with a symbol DIET CENTER on it, completed a weight goal chart with a symbol DIET CENTER on it, and was given a manual, "Weight Control Program for Women." She learned that the DIET CENTER advertised nationally for clients, and franchises attracted and contracted with clients. There were no professionals, doctors or nurses; the staff was all people who had been clients who lost weight.

"Who hates diet centers like doctors hate lawyers?" I had asked Kathy.

"Competent, well-trained internists and endocrinologists who treat obesity," she replied.

Dr. George Schneider at Beth Israel Hospital in Newark stiffened. "Change of personality and passing out can be caused by improper supervision of his diet program," he said. "It can lead to low potassium levels. Where did they take the gentleman after they got him out of the car?"

Medford General Hospital"

"How long was he there before he went to Crozer Chester?"

"Twelve hours sticks in my mind."

"Get me the hospital records and the Medford DIET CENTER records. Let me see what I can find."

A month passed. My telephone rang. Dr. Schneider was on the line. Josh Bryant's potassium level was precariously low, he said. "Dangerous, in fact."

"What does that mean?"

"You may have a case against the DIET CENTER. I have reached out to some colleagues. They say it's a shoddy operation. No doctors. No nurses. Run by people who buy franchises and use people who have lost weight to run the program. You have to get your client's records and their operation manuals before I can give you anything definitive."

If I just mailed a request for records, there was a good chance the records would disappear or be altered. If I started a lawsuit, I could send a subpoena. Failure to honor a subpoena was very risky. The suit charging the DIET CENTER, it's Medford franchise owner and its employees with negligent administration and supervision of Josh's diet program was filed. When Josh's records arrived two months later, I sent them to Dr. Schneider. Josh was still miraculously surviving, having had seven skin grafts. He was conscious and in command of his faculties. Josh was a miracle man, too.

Josh had begun the program on October 24 at 248 1/2 pounds and by November 9, he had lost 16 pounds, which Dr. Schneider believed was excessive and had caused a potassium deficiency. The contract documents prepared by the DIET CENTER required the franchise to follow "Guidelines, Policies and Procedures" that described "a quick weight loss program" where "People experience weight loss of 18 to 20 pounds in six weeks" and "Daily records of food intake and weight loss are absolutely necessary." These documents were emphatically confidential, to be read by people under contract to DIET CENTER or under employee contract only. This excluded counselors.

The purpose of the manual was "to educate franchisees about sales, business success, and dieting problems. It is to protect DIET CENTER from possible competitors. DIET CENTER sells a program that is non-medically supervised." My blood curdled.

Josh's records showed that without any doubt he was not monitored daily and was told to come three times a week, which he had done. Worse yet, the DIET CENTER knew that blacking out was a foreseeable result of its diet. The manual acknowledged that, "Many of our dieters are potassium deficient. It is good to have a bottle of potassium to sell. Some symptoms of potassium imbalance in the body are as follows: the person has no energy, may blackout, is weepy, has muscle weakness, and has a poor stomach and apathy. Potassium deficiency can impair muscle activity, slow heart beat, and in severe cases can cause failure of the respirator muscle."

The DIET CENTER did not provide for proper training of its counselors, and, in fact, created through its "Manual" a pattern of withholding information that was important to clients.

"Never show anyone's weight card to a friend, husband or wife."

"Overweight people are very sensitive and secret about their diets."

"If counselors have questions, they can ask you."

The manual, which Josh received, was deficient. It had no warning about a possible potassium deficiency. It called for a six-day a week counseling program during the "Reducing" phase. It did not reveal that a potassium supplement was available or could be bought.

Dr. Schneider was prepared to testify that the DIET CENTER did not properly educate or train counselors, that it did not properly educate or warn clients, that it withheld information that was important, that in Josh's case no notes were made, no graphing was done and that if the DIET CENTER had followed proper procedures accepted in the treatment of obesity, Josh would not have passed out, rolled across a sod farm and been engulfed in flames.

At Crozer Chester, Josh had made major progress, though he could barely walk. His physical therapy consisted of a nurse putting him on a bed and moving his arms and bending his joints while he screamed, "I hate this." "It hurts."

Josh was hospitalized at Crozer Chester Burn Center for fifty-one weeks, where he underwent sixty-two surgical procedures involving skin grafting. His automobile insurance company arranged for a temperature-controlled room to be built in Josh's house and for 24 hour nursing care. His policy provided for payment of medical bills and appliances. While Josh began to acclimate himself to life outside a hospital, I pushed forward with the lawsuit.

At depositions taken of the owner of the DIET CENTER, I asked, "Sir, did you prepare and read the information your company provided to its franchisees and clients?"

"No," he answered.

"Who did?"

"Our lawyers. I was under the impression that everything was proper and that we could not be sued."

I continued. "If you lose this case, will you sue your lawyer?"

The DIET CENTER owner replied, "Wouldn't you?"

I added a request for punitive damages to the lawsuit, which can be awarded if a person or corporation acts with willful, reckless and wanton disregard for the safety of others.

Some of Josh's closest friends stopped seeing him because it was too difficult for them. One admitted that he "couldn't stand to see Josh this way." But others, some Josh never thought of as close, actually visited and became good friends. When he was alone, he lay around the house, moping. Before the accident, one of his favorite hobbies was playing video games on his Nintendo system. Now, he was no longer able to play because the loss of his hands prevented him from using the controllers. He got around this limitation by playing games with Tim's son, who was seven years old at the time. They became a team. Josh would control the character in the game and tell his nephew where to go, what areas to avoid, and so on.

Eventually he got bored with Nintendo and Tim got him a computer. He was instantly hooked. Josh discovered the computer world, in its infancy, which brought a larger world into his house. During his waking hours, Josh plucked rapidly at the keys with the stub on his right hand. "The computer and the friends I meet there are what keep me alive," he said.

While Josh and millions of people were sharing information and playing games with their mouse, lawyer's organizations held conventions, meetings and seminars at which lawyers shared their knowledge. I met other lawyers who had handled burn cases and got a good sense of what kind of jury verdicts a case like Josh's would command. The range was from 10 to 25 million dollars. Insurance companies were holding conventions, too, aimed at educating their personnel to lobby Congress and state legislatures to change laws that provided injured people like Josh the wherewithal to deal with their tragedies. "Stop the Legal Lottery" campaigns sprung up across the country. Trial lawyers, like me, joined together to fight back, forming organizations like the Trial Lawyers of America, and the American Trial Lawyers Association.

Videotapes were used to record testimony of doctors and experts. Why not make a video of a day in the life of Josh Bryant? He could not appear in court.

Peter Antonuccio, a certified legal videographer, and I showed up at Josh's house at 7 a.m. and spent an entire day with Josh, his nurses, and a few friends. Peter edited six hours of videotape down to a film that took eleven minutes to watch. In the last scene, I looked squarely at the camera and said, "I represent Josh Bryant, who you will see was a functioning person until the DIET CENTER, its franchisor and employees so willfully and recklessly disregarded the safety warning in their own manuals. Now he is sentenced to a life of misery and challenges that you can see with your own eyes. I am authorized to accept 25 million dollars to settle this case. A jury could award much more. Additionally, punitive damages are sought against the owners of the DIET CENTER. Those damages are not covered by insurance. I urge you to act in good faith and provide the resources Josh will need to live the rest of his life."

I got an immediate response.

The DIET CENTER lawyer informed me that the insurance company would like to settle out of court. They offered 15 million dollars of insurance it had written to cover negligence of the DIET CENTER. The Medford DIET CENTER had a 2 million dollar policy. It, too, was tendered. I had seventeen million dollars on the table for Josh.

Josh, Tim and I discussed our options. We could go to trial and try to get a higher verdict, but that would risk a lower verdict. 17 million dollars was a lot of money, especially in rural New Jersey, where folks did not make large salaries. To many, 1 million dollars was a fortune. In the event a jury awarded many more millions, DIET CENTER could file for bankruptcy and wipe out the debt it would owe Josh.

Josh decided he wanted to be secure and move on.

Robert Voogt operated rehabilitation centers that treated spinal cord, brain injury and burn victims. His thirty years of experience taught him what people would need during their lifetime. I hired him to provide a life care plan that took into consideration a worse case scenario, that is, what Josh would need if his automobile insurance company went bankrupt and could not pay his medical bills for the rest of his life. The Pennsylvania Railroad had gone under. So could an insurance company.

Voogt determined that Josh had a life expectancy of 42.9 years from the date of the settlement. He predicted what Josh would need annually to pay general surgeons, physiatrists, orthopedic surgeons, and internists. He considered the cost of plastic surgery and respiratory treatments, both of which would probably be necessary in the future. He even estimated the cost of psychiatric care Josh and his family might need to adjust to his new life and help his family cope. If Josh were not physically challenged, he could do normal exercise to keep in shape. Voogt priced out the cost of physical rehabilitation, occupational therapy, recreational therapy and even vocational rehabilitation, given Josh's intelligence and drive. Other things to account for were a handyman, lawn care, a housekeeper and a van adapted with an independent mobility system for a wheelchair.

As I read the list of things Josh would need, I began to see what Josh's life was going to be like. A shower wheelchair. A wall-mounted personal shower. A personal whirlpool. A bionic arm. Wound cleaners. Wound gel. Band Aids. The list went on and on. Medicines. Pain killers. With 24 hours of daily support care, the sum of 9 million dollars would be necessary to fund Josh's needs.

Meetings with financial planners led to a plan which involved a diverse group of investments, including guaranteed annuities that would pay monthly sums that increased each year by three percent compounded, an insurance policy to provide a sum needed to pay estate taxes if Josh passed away, a portfolio of stocks and bonds managed by a national trust company, and cash that would permit Josh to buy a house large enough to house him and his brother's family so that he could not only have 24 hour a day nursing care but also the companionship of his family.

Six months after the settlement, monies in the neighborhood of 10 million were in place. Tim found the house they now live in. As Josh played games on the Internet more and more, he made friends with other people who were playing the same games. Eventually, he started to travel to Wisconsin and South Carolina to meet the friends that he had made and participate in computer game tournaments. Some of the people that he met turned out to have disabilities, too. At Christmas, a year after Josh moved into the house, he invited me to see what he had done.

"Do you want to see my game area?"

"Sure."

"I'll take you," Tim said. "Josh can't get down the stairs very well. We wanted Josh to be on the first floor, but he wanted privacy and the only place he could have that was upstairs."

The spacious basement was softly lit and covered with a blue carpet. The first thing that caught my eye was an enormous collection of miniature cars. There were all sorts of different makes, models, colors, years, and styles. Fords and Toyotas, convertibles and sedans, station wagons and 60s muscle cars neatly arranged on a series of shelves.

"Josh is a collector by nature," Tim explained. "He loves systematically organizing and categorizing all sorts of different things. The settlement money has helped him pursue these passions."

Another room had a large flat-screen TV with a Nintendo console system and tapes filling the shelves all around the room. "We all love to watch movies," Tim said. "So we use this room for parties and other events." It was rare to hear about a person with catastrophic injury hosting parties. "This is our pinball room," Tim said. He gestured at the machines lined up against the walls. Their colorful lighting gave the room a cozy glow. Tim proudly indicated a rare pinball machine that they had found in Austria.

"How does Josh play?"

On the ground beneath one of the machines was a board with buttons similar to those on the machine. "One of his friends set this up for him," said Tim. "Josh can push the buttons with his feet and play the games."

The beer cans that Josh had been collecting since he was a teenager were there too. Tim showed me an aluminum Miller Lite can with a distinctive twist-off top from the 1950s. "Many of the things Josh collects he was interested in before his accident. But after he received his settlement money, he was able to become serious about his collections. What you see represents how Josh spends his days."

At the end of 2002, Josh called to ask for the name of an accountant. The trust company had been filing his tax returns, but that year he had made over $200,000.

"Two hundred thousand?"

"Yup."

"You working? You have a job?"

Chuckling, Josh said, "Working, playing games." He got into The Sims Online, a computer game, and, "It grew into a business, gold farming for virtual currency and selling it on eBay for real money. It's very lucrative."

This I had to see.

A few days later, we sat in a room filled with monitors and computers. "I now have seventeen computers," Josh said. "I started with two. They more than paid for themselves with just the money I made selling the virtual currency. I would get up at ten in the morning and spend all day monitoring the computers, making sure that each character that I controlled in the game was doing the right thing." He chuckled. "Except to eat, I'd play all day. Around 2 a.m., I'd go to bed. Then I'd wake up the next day and repeat."

The Sims Online is a "game in which you control and develop a character and interact with other players. There is in-game currency with which you win prizes if you have enough of it. It's like if you shoot at stuffed animals on the boardwalk. If you hit them, you get tokens. Once you have enough, you trade them in for a reward. Now imagine if there were people willing to buy the tokens, so you could just play games all day and sell the tokens for a profit. Well, there were people playing this game willing to pay real money in exchange for the virtual currency."

My eyes rolled. I didn't understand a word Josh said.

"Let me show you how it works," Josh said.

Screens began to light up. He used a mouse with a cup attached to his left wrist. With the stub on his other hand, he typed on a keyboard faster than most people do who both hands in tact.

That fall, Josh invited me to the Eagles-Giants game. He had Eagles season tickets. And a brand new RV. "I bought it. Sixty-five thousand. A lot of money. But it helps manage my need for a controlled climate. We drive out to the stadium every Sunday in the fall when the Eagles have a game to tailgate and watch the game. We're there at 8 a.m. no matter what time the game begins and spend the whole day cooking steaks and burgers. If the weather's okay I sometimes make it inside to watch the game after the opening kickoff."

In July 2008, Josh has invited me to visit because he has something to discuss—something "private, that I don't want to talk about over the telephone." His home is in an upscale neighborhood of mini-mansions with gated driveways and manicured lawns. A fountain into which water flows from dark marble sculptures of lions stands in front of the house next door. Half of Josh's house is dominated by a long series of windows, ending in a three-car garage. An addition that will house a new bedroom, a video room and photography studio is covered by a protective layer of construction material—so Josh can have privacy and be on the first floor.

Tim, clad in a striped red Nike polo shirt and khaki shorts has a silver goatee on his round face and white hair falling to his shoulders. "Josh is coming down now," he said. "It's hard for him to get around, as he can't move his right leg very well. We had a lift built to make it easier for him to move around the house."

The house was a flurry of activity and commotion. Outside, on the deck, five men worked under the supervision of a foreman on the new addition. The sounds of their heavy boots thudding along the wooden planks as well as their hammering and sawing drifted inside. Past the deck was a swimming pool with a diving board and a fenced-in tennis court. A dining room with a large table was littered with children's games, boxes of clothes, and other assorted odds and ends. "The house is a real mess right now, what with all the construction work going on," Tim commented.

Josh, dressed in a yellow shirt with black and white stripes and dark blue sweatpants, walked slowly, gingerly placing one foot ahead of the other as he came through a kitchen door. His skin was taut, his neck veins prominent. Thin lips, slightly open, and downward-pointed, formed a mouth that looked as though it was fighting to suck in as much air as he could. His brown eyes were sad and weary, his dark, receding hair streaked with white. His arms were thin and veiny. His right arm ended in a pointy stub wrapped in bandages and covered by an elbow support. His left arm extended down to his hand, but instead of fingers, he had a meaty palm with one knuckled nub jutting out and several other small protrusions.

Tim brought me an iced tea in a Super Bowl XXXIX glass. He set a drink with a straw in it next to Josh. "It's been tough for Josh lately," Tim said, "especially now that he's had problems with his knee and requires medical attention for it. It's harder to find a vein on him than on a normal person." He flinched when he realized the implication of what he had said and quickly added, "Not that he's not normal."

Josh told me that he'd gone to the doctor because his left knee was swollen. He'd just found out he had a cancerous tumor. I may have to lose my leg." Then Josh grinned. "If I lose it, I can save twelve hours of nursing care because I won't need to have someone clean and put dressings on the open wounds that are on my leg. The grafts never took right."

Then he told me why he'd asked me to come.

"I want to talk to you about changing my will. As it is now, half goes to Tim and the other half goes into a trust for my two nephews. They get the money when they turn thirty-five." With the money he'd received fifteen years before, Josh had bought the house he lived in with his family for 1 million dollars. Annuities paid him $300,000 dollars a year, free of taxes, and his stocks and bonds had grown in value and were now worth 5 million dollars. His medical care was paid for with insurance, and extra items not covered were paid through a fund that had been set up in accordance with a life care plan.

"I want to take care of my family. That's for sure. Without them, I wouldn't have made it this far. But I have more than enough to do that. Tim is well off himself." Tim worked with a high tech firm and made a good salary. Josh's nephews were about to finish college. "I don't want my nephews to have too much money. In today's world, a little hunger isn't a bad thing."

"What are you thinking about doing?"

"Do you know about Bob Woodruff, the anchor on the World News Tonight?"

Woodruff, who suffered a brain injury as the result of an explosion he was in while covering the Iraq War, is the Christopher Reeve in the brain injury world.

"He set up a fund for people suffering from traumatic brain injury that promotes awareness and educates the general population about brain injury and raises funds to provide for the treatment of brain injury sufferers. I want to do the same thing for people who have suffered severe burns. These guys coming back from the wars are going to be as bad off as I am. Hopefully, Uncle Sam will take care of them, but…." Josh's eyes looked away. "After the settlement everybody becomes your 'friend,' Josh said with a sarcastic smile. "Relatives, friends, even some of the aides that looked after me thought that they were entitled to a cut."

Tim added, "But that doesn't mean that Josh hasn't been very generous." While Josh blushed, he described how his brother gave his old house to his sister, paid for Tim's children's college, even gave money to some of his aides who needed help with medical bills.

"The money has enabled us to take trips as a family," Josh said. "We went to Las Vegas last year, Tim's family and I. "The most difficult part has been managing the settlement correctly," Josh said. "We set up a life care plan, investing the money in US Trust, the company that was eventually bought by Bank of America. It grew for a while and even made a sizable profit, but we lost a substantial amount in the dotcom crash. Luckily, the money we lost was mostly profit and not the principal, so we learned from our mistakes and invested it in less risky options. Currently, half of it is in stocks and half in mutual funds. The annuity system is wonderful."

Without the money, Josh would have been dependent on his brother and sister. I know people who get very little help from their insurance companies," he said. "Some who are severely handicapped only get one hour of help a day. Then of course, there's this house. It is a very nice house, but we bought it using some of my settlement money so that my brother and his family could live with me and help look after me."

"I function as Josh's caretaker," said Tim. "It's what I've been doing since the accident. Even so many years later, there are still things that Josh only trusts me to do for him. Before we bought this house, when we lived separately, I felt guilty all the time. If I was looking after Josh, I felt guilty for neglecting my wife and kids. If I was with my family, I felt guilty for neglecting Josh's needs. Taking care of Josh has become a major part of my life—there have only been a handful of times in the last 17 years that my wife and I have had time alone for ourselves. Our current arrangement is the best of both worlds. But it would not have been possible without the settlement."

When Tim walked me to the car later, he said, "He was just a typical guy in his 20s. There are definitely things that he can't do now that he used to do, but he has also done things since the accident that he wouldn't have had the opportunity to do before."

Most seriously injured people reminisced about their lives before the accident. Unlike them, Josh did not seem bitter or unable to let go of the past, but, instead, looked forward and continued to lead a fulfilling life. I thought my next task was to help Josh create his legacy.

9. CLOSING STATEMENT

When you go to into the voting booth to exercise your right to choose those who represent you in a democratic society, you are one of many. Rarely does your vote make a difference. When a juror votes, his or her vote is one of six, or at most twelve, a vote that is important to the citizens whose fate has been put in a jury's hands. A juror leaves a courthouse and returns to his or her life, leaving in his or her wake a decision that affects the citizens who appeared before them for the rest of his or her life. Oftentimes, the decision brings about changes that give us safer cars, roads, bicycle helmets, and factories.

During the 1960s and 1970s, Congress passed consumer protection laws, giving people the right to sue for damages if the business produced or sold a defective or dangerous product. By definition, a tort requires that those responsible or at fault for harming others compensate the victims with money to make up for loss of income, medical expenses and pain and suffering. The tort system is criticized for its alleged high cost and inefficiency, but these laws helped Angelo Angarone, Josh Bryant and thousands more right a wrong.

The jury trial guaranteed by our Constitution is in jeopardy from tort reform movements in federal and state legislatures that are winning battles to restrict and limit victims' rights to sue for damages. In 1774, John Adams said, "Representative government and trial by jury are the heart and lungs of liberty. Without them we have no other fortification against being ridden like horses, fleeced like sheep, worked like cattle, and fed and clothed like swine and hounds." A jury trial is not the only means to fortify those people who are a shadow of what they were a millisecond ago, but it is and must be the bastion of last resort.

An old lawyer "story" goes like this. The plaintiff's lawyer tells one side of the story. The defendant's lawyer tells the other side. Courtroom drama envelops you. How many times have I been afraid of an unsympathetic jury, of ending up with nothing, even if my client had been wronged and needed money to survive? How often have I asked myself to calculate damages for pain and suffering? How many times have I said to myself that a jury's decision that was half of what it awarded, or double or triple the award, would have made just as much sense?

Proponents of abolishing juries in civil cases argue that a jury composed of ordinary people does not have the expertise to make a determination as to how much money a seriously injured person needs to continue with his or her life. The legal system in which seriously injured people find themselves is far from perfect.

How did I lose the foot doctor's case? Because a lawyer banged his head against a courtroom wall and said, "I'm not brain-injured?" No. I lost because I was not perfect, because I did not present testimony from witnesses who knew the doctor before and after the crash. In interview after interview with jurors who have decided cases differently from how I would have decided, I listened to reasonable views that considered elements of the case that I had overlooked.

My experience has taught me that if cases are well presented by both sides, the jury listens and tells the truth. The jury usually gets "the story" right. The seriously injured person survives the drama.

Ronald Reagan told a story that became a rallying cry to groups that called themselves "tort reformers." As Reagan told it, Charles Bigbee was making a telephone call in a public phone booth when a drunk driver crashed into the booth. The injured man sued the telephone company and won a huge settlement. What Reagan didn't tell was the "rest of the story."

Yes, Charles Bigbee had been in a telephone booth in 1974, thirteen years before. Yes, he was making a call. Yes, a speeding car did approach the booth. Bigbee saw the car and tried to flee, but the door jammed, trapping him.

Now for the "rest of the story:" A year and a half before Bigbee entered it, the whole telephone booth had been destroyed by another car. The telephone company installed a new booth but simply replaced the damaged door without putting in new hinges, so the door would not open. So it makes sense that the telephone company settled with Bigbee for $500,000.

Who hasn't heard about the 3 million dollar verdict against McDonalds? How could someone who spilled coffee on herself win a lawsuit? Trial evidence tells us how.

The car in which 79 year old Stella Liebeck was riding with her grandson stopped at a McDonald's in Albuquerque, New Mexico. She bought a cup of coffee. Her grandson pulled to the curb so she could put cream and sugar in the coffee. The car, a Ford Probe, did not have a cup holder, so she put the cup between her legs and took off the lid. The coffee spilled on her lap and she began to scream. She suffered third degree burns on her legs, was hospitalized for a week and had painful skin grafts, which left her permanently scarred.

McDonalds offered her $800, not the $20,000 her medical care cost, so she went to a lawyer. Her lawyer found out that McDonald's restaurants served coffee at 195-205 degrees Fahrenheit, a temperature high enough to peel skin. At the trial, jurors heard evidence that McDonald's had received seven hundred complaints of serious burns from its coffee over three years. Outraged, jurors awarded Stella Liebeck money for her pain and suffering and medical bills, reduced the award by 20% for her own carelessness, and then added $2,700,000 for punitive damages, two days' profits from McDonald's coffee sales at the time. McDonald's cooled its coffee to 158 degrees and then Stella Liebeck and McDonald's settled for substantially less than the verdict after the trial judge reduced the punitive award to $480,000. A condition of the settlement prohibited both parties from informing the public what the actual settlement was.

A lawyer advocating for those who deserve just compensation confronts the myth of Stella Liebeck and her 3 million dollars. This myth is hard to dispel because the media is unable to tell the "rest of the story."

To chase away the Stella Liebeck myth and jump over the hurdle of misinformation, I tell jurors that I know what they have heard and seen about lawsuits and request that they not make up their minds before they hear the "rest of the story."

I advocate mediation to make the legal process more equitable for people with catastrophic injuries. A trained mediator knows about settlements and verdicts in similar cases from court records and publications that regularly report them, which under current rules of evidence jurors are prohibited from knowing. Before mediation, plaintiff and defense experts can talk to each other so that they can understand their differences of opinion as to the diagnosis of the patient and work toward a mutual understanding and recommendation that fulfills the victim's needs. Mediation leads to more cases ending in settlements and helps avert the bitterness and acrimony that result when cases get to court.

A settlement ensures that people get at least a reasonable amount of money for care, rather than being unable to pay for their bills and medical care if a jury finds against them. People get validation from a settlement, which tells them "yes" it is recognized that you have suffered a tremendous injury that will alter the rest of your life." That, in and of itself, creates an opportunity for a person to move on with his or her life.

A trial should be a last resort. Medical and life care experts charge high fees to appear in court or testify by video. People, already seriously injured, are in a strange setting, facing skilled defense attorneys who often accuse them of causing or faking their injuries and symptoms and listening to defense experts downplay the extent of their injuries. After a verdict is handed down, there is the expense of appeals, collecting payment and fighting with insurance companies. The post-trial process creates more angst and anxiety, slowing down the adjustment process.

After a mediated settlement or a trial, people still need the continued emotional support that lawyers provide. People fight to adjust to an altered and often cold world, one where they struggle to find companionship and understanding. Josh's legacy will be a fund to provide psychological help to burn victims and their families. Bob Woodruff and the Buonoconti family have created funds for brain-injured and paralyzed victims, respectively. Publicly funded programs should be set up for all seriously injured victims.

For the millions who survive catastrophic injuries, medical services are a diffuse patchwork of physical and mental health programs, educational and social services. In January 2006, ABC TV anchorman Bob Woodruff, embedded with an infantry division in Iraq, had his head above the hatch of an armored vehicle when an improvised explosive device (IED) detonated. A neurosurgical team at a nearby field hospital removed a portion of his skull to reduce pressure from brain swelling. Evacuated to a military hospital in Germany, he received the most comprehensive rehabilitation services money could buy.

In 2009, British actress Natasha Richardson fell and hit her head on a ski slope in Canada. Doctors at a nearby hospital did not have the knowledge and equipment to perform the emergency surgery that saved Bob Woodruff's life—and the lives of Amber and Barbara, Terry and Andy, Josh and Skylar. No helicopter was available to fly Richardson to a hospital where those resources were available. She died a day later from pressure caused by bleeding of the brain that could have been prevented by a competent neurosurgical team.

Seriously injured people, citizens and especially brave soldiers who have served us, must have the resources they need so they have a chance to be a Woodruff and not a Richardson. Medical care after an injury must be given by specialists trained in treating traumatic spinal cord, brain and burn injuries.

Andy's parents wished that doctors, trained in how to treat specific ills, focused more on the overall well-being of their patients and strived to understand each one's unique background. "Sometimes," as they said, "the treatment should be more than medical."

I advocate that states create one state agency to plan for and effectuate catastrophic injury care. Programs to train emergency staff, chemical dependency professionals, vocational rehabilitation specialists and mental health professionals must be established. Universities and community colleges can create courses to provide rehabilitation education directed at adults and school age children. Funds from a portion of motor vehicle violation fines for speeding, drunk driving and seat belt offenses, fines from Occupational Safety and Health Act violations, and punitive damages awards can offset the costs. States should rely less on facility-based services like those offered Terry at Health North and more on individual services like those offered Amber at the Lynch Home.

Affordable housing programs similar to those for senior citizens and low and moderate-income families must provide for special needs. Where appropriate, state and local governments should fund programs to empower victims to make choices for themselves about job interests and capability.

I advocate that stem cell researchers receive funding now that President Barack Obama has encouraged the use of adult stem cells. During the past eight years, while George W. Bush was president, stem cell research was banned. Right to Life advocates opposed stem cell research, saying that stem cells derived from early human embryos and aborted fetuses was a form of murder, the killing of an innocent human being, no matter how small. In 1998, stem cells were isolated from human embryos and aborted fetuses. With stem cell research, important knowledge can be gained about embryonic development, curing spinal cord injuries and diseases like Parkinson's, Alzheimer's and diabetes.

The insurance industry has to promote reforms, too. No-fault insurance, not only for automobile accidents, but also to employees through employer health plans, should be required to be offered. Health and auto insurance companies ought to offer coverage provisions for inpatient and outpatient coverages for therapies delivered in acute care and rehabilitation hospitals. Health Maintenance Organizations (HMO's) and private plans such as Point of Provider Organizations (PPO's) should provide for comprehensive rehabilitation services.

Currently, there is no economic incentive for an insurance company to accept a claim as being valid. The more claims they try to deny and fight in court, the more money they save in the long run.

I advocate a co-sharing plan in which states create a catastrophic injury fund available to those without medical and financial support. This would spread the risk for a catastrophic injury claim across several insurance companies.

I advocate that structured settlements, approved by the court, should be mandatory in catastrophic injury cases. Praise is due Congress for its wisdom in creating laws that have permitted settlements to be structured, free of federal and state income taxes, protecting vulnerable victims from dissipating a fund that will need to last the rest of their lives. People for whom I have battled successfully have, at times, disappointed me, treating their victory as though they had won a lottery and the money awarded as misery money, spending it foolishly, or giving it away to family and friends who take advantage of their vulnerability.

You have walked in the shoes of people and those whose lives they have touched on these pages or in real life. You have felt the repercussions: memory deficits, judgment changes, loss of mobility, substance abuse, divorce, loss of friends, and need for constant supervision, help managing money, household chores, even bathing. You have seen that seriously injured people need and want good relationships with friends and family, respect, dignity, the opportunity to develop and use whatever competence they have left, the opportunity to contribute to their community, make choices for their future and control their lives and the services they need. You have witnessed families exhaust resources and pay a high psychological and financial price. You have witnessed their voyage through the legal system, imperfect as it is, but still the best on earth.

Now that you know the "rest of the story," you can be a spark, igniting a flame that casts light on those in our midst who are too often invisible and without a voice. Being an advocate for them, you can influence public officials to create jobs that assist people—seriously brain injured, paralyzed or burned—and their families, to build housing that meets peoples' needs, and urge those whose efforts are endemic to them to mend the holes they poke into the fabric of our society.

The "rest of the story" will be told in the years ahead. You can be part of it.

TAKE AWAYS

ASK THE RIGHT QUESTIONS.

Bobbie's case launched my career as a trial lawyer, representing people who suffered spinal cord, burn and brain injuries. Each type of injury demands medical and legal specialists devoted to that injury. A client must never lose sight of the fact that he or she has only one chance to seek compensation that must last the rest of his or her life. Because people who have been seriously injured do not know what questions to ask before they retain a lawyer, make sure the seriously injured person knows the answers to these questions.

How many cases like mine have you handled over the past five years?

If a lawyer has handled less than ten, be polite and search for another lawyer.

How many cases have you tried in court and received a jury verdict involving injuries like mine?

If a lawyer has tried less than five or if two or more were losses, be polite and search for another lawyer.

What percentage of your practice is devoted to cases and injuries like mine?

If the answer is less than 50%, be polite and search for another lawyer.

What seminars or conferences have you attended over the past five years where presentations were given about injuries like mine?

If the answer is less than three, be polite and search for another lawyer.

Will you be willing and able to spend as much as $100,000 to investigate, prepare and present my case as part of the contingent fee agreement?

If a lawyer is not willing or able to do it, be polite and search for another lawyer.

What type of experts do you anticipate you will need to help you with the analysis and preparation of my case?

If a lawyer will not give you that information, be polite and search for another lawyer.

AFTER YOU HAVE FOUND THE RIGHT LAWYER.

When you are satisfied that you have found the "right lawyer," you will question whether the contingent fee of 33 1/3% is fair. Would you be able to pay your advocate for the services you are receiving or have received? The contingent fee makes it possible for your advocate not only to help you but also to help others whose causes appear hopeless.

As you embark on your journey for justice, make sure:

1. You have a clear understanding of the steps your advocate must take to win in court.

2. Your advocate is fulfilling his or her promise to be equipped to investigate and advise you about social and financial concerns you have.

3. You communicate to your lawyer stories that will enable others to understand what it is like to walk in your shoes.

4. Who are the members of your legal team? What are their roles?

5. What must your legal team prove to a court and jury to win your case?

6. What is your legal team doing to help you deal with stress, anger and frustration?

7. What up-to-date legal research tools does your legal team use?

8. What kinds of experts does your case require?

9. Do you know how much money you will need to satisfy your living needs after your case is over?

10. How will you determine if a settlement or verdict is fair?

Make sure your legal team:

Helps you with your feelings of frustration, helplessness and anger.

Discusses with you your medical and financial needs.

Tells you the strengths and weaknesses of your case.

Communicates with your caregivers to be sure they are teaching you to live with your injury.

Communicates with your caregivers to be sure they are developing strategies to cope with your deficits.

CHECK IT OUT.

What would my family do if I got into a situation where I was unable to provide for them?

If you, or a family member, was in a horrible accident, who would pay the medical bills?

What would happen to your children if you or your spouse was not here to care for them?

Do I have disability insurance? What does it cover?

Should I start thinking about long term care insurance?

Do I have an up-to-date will?

Does your family know your wishes?

Is there a living will? Is it being honored?

If I needed it, could I get into my retirement account? If I drained it, what would I do?

What if I were Bobbie or Skylar? Could my family handle it? Do they have the resources to do so?

What resources do you or a loved one have to give birth to a "new you" or "new me"?

Who would be appointed guardian for you or a loved one? Should someone else be named?

EMOTIONAL I.Q. TEST.

If you were normally against personal injury lawsuits, would you contact a lawyer if your child was seriously injured?

If you were dating someone for three years and they suffered a serious injury, would you stay with them?

If you were the one who suffered a serious injury and your friends eventually stopped having contact with you, what would you do to keep your spirits up?

Do you think you could handle your new way of life as well as the clients whose stories you have read?

Imagine yourself unable to recognize your loved ones and friends on a daily basis, how would you feel living in a world filled with strangers, including you?

Picture yourself questioning people around you as your ability to trust others has been taken away from you as you can no longer trust your memory to guide you. Is it possible to live a grounded life?

At this point in your life, whom can you trust?

Although normal and healthy outwardly, inwardly you are lost, scared and confused as your perception has been altered by no fault of your own. Who is going to understand what you feel internally when externally there are no apparent injuries to explain your perception and paranoia?

Think about being labeled a fake because you feel your injuries have impacted your life to the point you want others to be aware and informed about closed head injuries, but to do so, you are subjected to grueling tests and questioned about your integrity. At this moment in time you must make a decision whether or not to proceed with litigation, or crawl in some dark recess of your mind where only you and you alone live with the daily confusion that trauma has caused and the permanent changes wrought by the trauma.

If your life were altered permanently, would you have regrets of your past, or would the memory loss make you have regrets for your future?

How do you learn to look forward without constantly thinking about, and being emotionally hamstrung by the past?

How do you allay the guilt felt by a close friend who may have contributed to your injury, even though they were not at fault and maintain a close relationship with that person?

Without sounding defensive about it, how do you deal with people who resent you because they think you received too much money?

How do you know when you are explaining your problems to someone, if they really understand you?

DO'S

Keep a daily record of problems you encounter.

See a doctor to discuss handling of depression.

Put aside pride, guilt, and resentment in order to act properly and intelligently and seek help from competent professionals.

Seek truthful and accurate information about the extent of your injury and the financial burdens involved in living out the rest of your life.

Try to arrive at realistic expectations as the amount of money your case is worth.

Think about the risks of not settling your case.

Think about your financial future.

Plan what to do if you receive a sizable judgment.

Find people you can trust to look after your well-being.

Look for a meaningful job, no matter how menial, that you can do for pay or as a volunteer.

Locate support groups in your town or community.

SOURCES

During my career, I have used many books to learn about catastrophic injuries and called upon organizations for help.

I am sure that in opening and closing statements I delivered in court that I mouthed the words of authors. Their words became etched in my mind as if they were my own. While I can not attribute some of the observations I have made in this book to a particular author, I would be remiss if I did not make reference to many of them and suggest that lawyers, doctors, caregivers, victims and their families and my readers read the following books and contact the following organizations.

Karen Brennan, Being With Rachel: A Personal Story of Memory and Survival. W.W. Norton and Company, 2002.

Karen Brennan tells the story of how she dealt with being the sole caretaker of her 24 year-old daughter after she suffered a traumatic brain injury in a motorcycle accident.

Beverly Bryant, In Search of Wings: A Journey Back From Traumatic Brain Injury. Wings Publishing. 1992.

Bryant accounts how she faced her traumatic brain injury and fought to overcome the challenges presented by TBI.

Donald J. Lloyd, Shannon L. Kehoe and Susan E. Lloyd, Smile and Jump High! A True Story of Overcoming Traumatic Brain Injury. Starlight Press, 2001.

A step-by-step account of how one family deals with family member's traumatic brain injury told through journals and diaries.

Douglas J. Mason and Gottfried Jean-Louis, The Mild Traumatic Brain Injury Workbook: Your Program for Regaining Cognitive Function and Overcoming Emotional Pain. New Harbinger Publications, 2004.

Provides self-help strategies to help brain injury patients to counteract emotional problems and regain some of the cognitive skills and brain functions that they have lost as a result of head injury.

Claudia Osborn, Over My Head: A Doctor's Own Story of Head Injury From Inside Looking Out. Andrews McMeel Publishing, 2000.

A doctor's account of her brain injury from a motorcycle accident. Intended for patients and their families and health care professionals.

Bruce Stern and Jeffrey Brown, Litigating Brain Injuries, ATLA Press 2006.

A brain injury lawyer and a lawyer – physician share strategies to be used in court.

Cara L. Swanson, I'll Carry The Fork! Recovering A Life After Brain Injury. Rising Star Press, 1999.

Swanson shares her own personal brain injury experience and her efforts to recover her life after her injury as a way to inspire other brain injury victims.

J.J. Walsh, Understanding Paraplegia, Tavistock Publications, 1964.

A physician's description of what a spinal cord victims experiences and the problems that must be overcome.

William J. Winslade, Confronting Traumatic Brain Injury: Devastation, Hope, and Healing. Yale University Press, 1999.

Winslade presents accounts of brain injury victims in an attempt to bring TBI and the alarming figures concerning how many people suffer from it to the attention of the public.

Helpful organizations:

Brain Injury Association
105 North Alfred Street
Alexandria, Virginia 22314
800 444 6443
www.biausa.org

National Spinal Cord Injury Association
1 Church Street #600
Rockville, Maryland 20850
800 962 9629
www.spinalcord.org

American Burn Association
625 N. Michigan Avenue
Suite 2550
Chicago, Illinois 60611
312 642 9130
www.americanburn.org

Association of Rehabilitation Nurses
4700 West Lake Avenue
Glenview, Illinois 60025-1485
800 229 7530
www.rehabnurse.org

The Association for Persons with Severe Handicaps
29 West Susquehanna Avenue Suite 210
Baltimore, Maryland 21204
410 828 8274
www.TASH.org

American Physical Therapy Association
111 North Fairfax Street
Alexandria, Virginia 22314
800 999 2782
www.APTA.org

Association for Children and Adults with Learning Disabilities
4156 Library Road
Pittsburgh, Pennsylvania 15234
412 341 1515
www.LDAAmerica.org

American Occupational Therapy Association
4720 Montgomery Lane
P.O. Box 31220
Bethesda, Maryland 20824
301 652 2682
www.AOTA.org

All of the organizations I have offered you will refer you to appropriate resources in your location.

ACKNOWLEDGMENT

Alexander Friedman, a Dartmouth college student who interned with me, earned my heartfelt thanks. Alex arranged and attended most of the interviews, which became the basis for this book. Without Alex's enthusiasm and dedication, I question whether I would have completed this book.

To the Rich family, especially Nina, I give hugs and kisses.

A special thanks goes to Dr. Jeffrey Brown, who gave me his time and insights.

Thank you to Tom, Ed, and Polly Meara, Irv and Tillie Spetgang, Meridith Stevens and Jim Pirone, Betty and Harry Gurke, Michael Terreri, Mary Trapani, Betsy Braun, Frank and Brian Rich, Patti Hughes, Michael, Catherine and Frank Ianno, David and Barbara Laurenti, Debbie Hughes, Jeff Richardson, Jackie Gufrovich, Michael Terreri, Edward Clark, Eddie Piotroski, John Simpson, and those who asked to remain anonymous.

Many many thanks go to Louise Bernikow for editing the stories, giving them structure and energy and to Gary Stoltman, a challenged paraplegic, who read the stories and added insights.

Nancy Karlosky and Florance Churchill, to whom this book is dedicated, were at my side for forty-five and twenty-five years, respectively. They provided facts and memories that had vanished from my mind.

Debbie Best was my life support when my mastery of Word reached its limits.

Without the support and encouragement of my colleagues at Stark and Stark, I would not have had the time and opportunity to write this book. Without the help of the lawyers and legal assistants referred to in the stories, I would not have been able to jump the hurdles for those who put their lives in my hands.

As always, Ellen has supported my efforts to make a difference in people's lives.

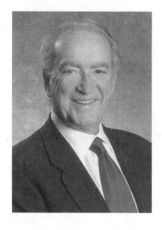

ABOUT THE AUTHOR

One of the nation's leading lawyers in the field of accident law, Albert Stark has pioneered the use of video and demonstrative evidence in the courtroom. Victories led to safer cars, bicycles, recreational vehicles, industrial equipment and roads. He has received awards recognizing his expertise, advocating for people with brain, spinal cord and burn injuries.

He is an effective speaker, has hosted radio and television programs, and has written articles on the use of video in the courtroom, brain injuries, unsafe roads and mediation. He is the author of Beyond The Bar — Challenges in a Lawyer's Life, (2002) and A War Against Terror through My Lens (2006).

A graduate of Dartmouth College and the University of Pennsylvania Law School, Stark is a partner in the Stark & Stark law firm with offices in Princeton and Marlton, New Jersey, Philadelphia and Bucks County, Pennsylvania and New York City. He practices in the firm's Personal Injury Group where he concentrates on seriously injured clients, particularly those who suffer from severe brain, spinal cord and burn injuries.

Stark is a member of the Mercer County, New Jersey, and American Bar Associations. He had been qualified as an Arbitrator with the United States District Court and has been certified by the Supreme Court of New Jersey as a Certified Civil Trial Attorney. Prior to joining Stark & Stark, he was a Ford Foundation Fellow and an Assistant to the Governor of New Jersey.

The New Jersey Trial Lawyers Association recognized Mr. Stark with its Trial Bar Award in 2000. He has been named a Super Lawyer and one the Best Lawyers in America.

He lives with his wife, Ellen, in Princeton.